I0039888

Nelson Williams and his Descendants

Three Generations from Maine, USA to New Brunswick, Canada and Beyond

Compiled by

Jeffrey Nelson Williams

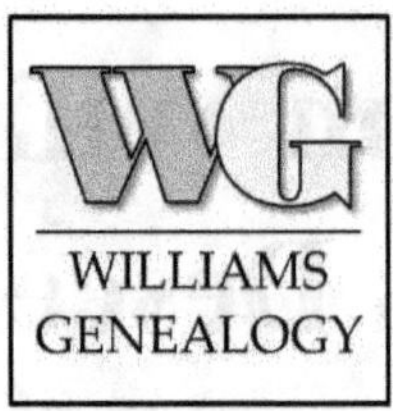

Published by Williams Genealogy
San Jose, California
www.wmsgen.com

Printed by CreateSpace

First Printing August 2017

International Standard Book Number 978-0-578-19479-0

Acknowledgements

Putting together a book like this cannot be done without help and the inspiration from others. There are so many in the genealogy community who have taken time to gather and preserve the documents of the past and make them available to others. Without their efforts and generosity so much of our history would be lost and my job of assembling family history into a book like this would be nearly impossible.

During the process of gathering the information included in this book I had the pleasure of twice visiting the New Brunswick, Canada area. The amount of support and assistance I received from everyone that I met there was beyond my expectations. I do want to take this opportunity to extend my gratitude to a few individuals and groups that really gave me a helping hand. First my cousin Helene Comeau Williams, whom I first met on initial trip to the City of Saint John, thank you for sharing all of your research and knowledge of our extended New Brunswick family and for your on-going friendship. To May Hayes at Cedar Hill-Greenwood Cemetery in Saint John West, your patience in answering my many inquiries regarding my family who are buried in one of your cemeteries is much appreciated. Kudos to the team in the Reference Department at the Central Branch of the Saint John Free Public Library, especially Jody Osiki who helped me research microfilmed newspaper records for obituaries and death notices. For providing me with family information from Northumberland County, New Brunswick I want to thank Sarah Wallace, Archivist at the United Church of Canada Maritime Conference; Wendell Gregan, DLM, with the Millerton Pastoral Charge; Jennifer Wilcox, Library Director, at the Chatham Public Library; and Judy Vautour with the Miramichi Branch of the New Brunswick Genealogical Society. And, to several of my cousins in Canada who patiently took the blind phone calls from some guy in California claiming to be related to them, thank you for hearing me out and sharing your family history.

When conducting genealogy research I have found that one is always walking a fine line between an engrossing hobby and a complete obsession. I especially have to thank my wife, Jackie, for her infinite support and patience with the many, many hours that I spend engrossed in my family history research and for frequently reminding me that I need to “get my head out of the graveyard and rejoin the living”.

August 2017

About this Book

ORGANIZATION - This book has been organized into sections by generation. "Section I – The First Generation" documents the life of Nelson Williams, "Section II – The Second Generation" addresses the children of Nelson Williams and "Section III – The Third Generation" covers the grand-children of Nelson Williams.

At the beginning of each Section, as shown in the example below, there is an index that allows the reader to follow the line of descendants from Nelson Williams to what page their biography is located in that section.

III

The Third Generation

The Grand Children of Nelson Williams

FORMAT – Each section contains a biographical and historical summary of the descendant's life from birth to death, as the information available allows. Wherever possible anecdotal information has been added to the historical facts listed.

NAMES – Throughout this book when documenting their history I have used an individual's legal given first and middle name, or middle initial. It should also be noted that a person's legal name may occasionally differ from the name they were most commonly known as. Examples of this could be for a woman with the legal name of Elizabeth who was commonly known as Betsey or Eliza. Or for someone who was commonly known by their middle name such as Charles Grierson who was known by many as Grierson. Legal names have been obtained from birth, marriage and death records.

USE OF *ITALICS* - When listing the children of a family member you will notice that some of their names are in *italics,* as seen in the example below.

John Nelson	b. October 19, 1842	d. March 22, 1924
David	*b. April 14, 1844*	*d. January 28, 1845*
Silas M.	b. July 15, 1847	d. December 24, 1918
Eliza Ann	b. 1849	d. September 21, 1882
Phoebe Elizabeth	b. September 24, 1852	d. December 1, 1915
Benjamin Franklin	b. August 24, 1855	d. December 5, 1918

For those individuals whose name is listed in *italics*, such as David in the example above, you will find that information for them will stop in the section where they are first listed. The reason behind this is (a) they died in their youth, (b) they died as young adults and were never married and/or were without issue, or (c) sufficient information regarding their life and death could not be found to support writing an individual biography.

LOCATIONS IN SAINT JOHN – New Brunswick is one of Canada's three Maritime Provinces. The Province itself contains fifteen counties which are primarily used as an organization for the registry of real estate. Saint John, one of New Brunswick's counties, also contains the City of Saint John which can cause some confusion when conducting genealogy research. When one finds a reference indicating "Saint John" it is not always readily apparent if it was for the City or County. Also adding to the challenge is the fact that over the years the boundaries of the City of Saint John grew and its' geography has expanded to include towns such as Portland, Lancaster and the Parrish of Simonds. And if that wasn't enough to cause some potential confusion, the City of Saint John is also a city of neighborhoods. Residents often identified themselves with their neighborhood and past census and legal documents identified individuals with their particular geographic area such as Carlton, Fairville, Indiantown, etc. Finally, there is one more twist. In recent times the geographic designations of Saint John West and East Saint John have also come into use.

So to assist the reader with the local geography I have grouped the historic neighborhoods and towns with the more recent designations they are associated with.

- **Saint John West** – contains Carlton (Albert, Brooks and Guy's Wards), Fairville, Greenhead, Lancaster, Milford, South Bay and Randolph.
- **East Saint John** – contains Loch Lomond and Simonds.

The remaining towns and neighborhoods, including Dukes, Kings, Princes, Queens, Sydney and Wellington Wards, as well as Indiantown, Millidgeville, Mount Pleasant and Portland may also be referred to as "**Saint John City**" in this book.

SOURCES - At the end of each person's biography the source documents used to support the individual's life history are listed. All source documents have been reviewed by the author prior to inclusion. If a document, or an independent verifiable source, has not been found to support a "Birth" or a "Marriage" fact, that source area will be left blank. If the "Death" and/or "Graveyard" source area is blank it can mean one of two things (a) a document or independent verifiable source has not been found or (b) the person is still living.

PERSON INDEX - As given names may often be repeated across generations, next to each person's name their year of birth and death has been listed to make it easier for the reader to find the summary for a specific individual they are looking for.

CORRECTIONS – I have done my best to transcribe and interpret individual's information from the available documentation. However, the reader may find unintentional errors or omissions. Please send any corrections you may have to editor@wmsgen.com.

Table of Contents

I

The First Generation:

Nelson Williams

Nelson Williams

(1807 -)

Nelson, the second child of Daniel Williams and Abigail Maynard, was born in Bingham, Somerset, Maine, USA on July 1, 1807. He was a direct descendant of Richard Williams and his wife Frances Deighton who first established his direct Williams family line in North America around 1635/1636 when they emigrated from Gloucester, England to Taunton, Bristol, Massachusetts, USA.

Sometime after it was published in 1828, Nelson passed on a bible he once owned to his sister Abigail Maynard. This is believed to have occurred sometime between 1828 and 1838, the year his sister was married. Below is a copy of Nelson's signature from the front cover sheet of that bible.

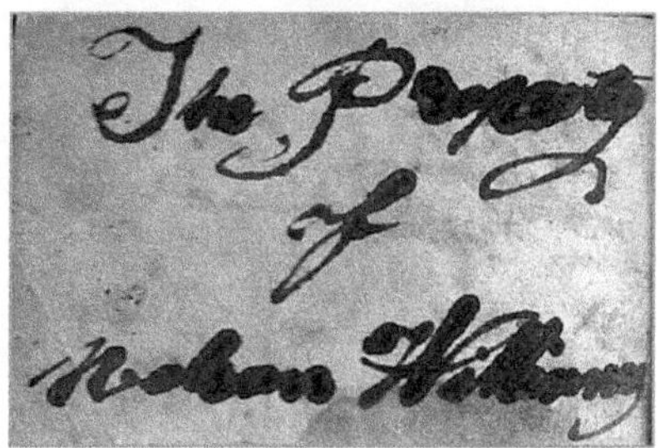

Nelson Williams' signature from the Williams/Briggs Family Bible
(From the collection of Jeffrey N. Williams and Jacqueline Pon Williams)

When the 1830 United States Federal Census was taken Nelson was recorded as living with his parents in Township No. 1, 4th Range, East Kennebec River, Somerset, Maine.

At age thirty-two, on June 6, 1839, Nelson was married to Elizabeth Dunham, age twenty-one, in Lancaster, Saint John, New Brunswick, Canada by Reverend Wilson of the Church of Scotland. Elizabeth, born in 1812, was the daughter of David Alston Dunham and Mary Ann Cathline of Lancaster. The exact date and place of her birth has not been found.

It should be noted that in the Marriage Register for Saint John County, New Brunswick the transcriber listed Nelson's name as "William N. Williams". This is the only official document that has been found that lists his name that way and is believed to be a transposition error.

After their marriage Nelson and Elizabeth traveled back to Maine and made Somerset County their home where they were listed as living in Township No. 1, 4th Range, East Kennebec River when the 1840 United States Federal Census was taken. In that census Nelson was recorded as "employed in agriculture".

During their marriage Nelson and Elizabeth had six children.

John Nelson	b. October 19, 1842	d. March 22, 1924
David D.	*b. April 16, 1844*	*d. January 28, 1845*
Silas M.	b. July 15, 1847	d. December 24, 1918
Eliza Ann	b. 1849	d. August 9, 1882
Phoebe Elizabeth	b. September 24, 1852	d. December 1, 1915
Benjamin Franklin	b. August 24, 1855	d. December 5, 1938

The second child of Nelson and Elizabeth, David D., died on January 28, 1845 at the young age of nine months and twelve days old. The cause and place of his death have not been found. He was buried in the Moscow Union Cemetery in Moscow, Somerset, Maine.

Gravestone for David D. Williams
(Photograph Courtesy of "maine" at Find A Grave)

Sometime in-between the birth of their daughters Eliza Ann in 1849 and Phoebe Elizabeth in 1852, Nelson and Elizabeth moved their family to Saint John County, New Brunswick, Canada where Elizabeth was born. This was the start of the extensive Williams family line in the New Brunswick area.

The 1863-1864 Hutchinson's Saint John Directory listed Nelson as living in Portland, Saint John, New Brunswick at Straight Shore opposite Ruddock's Yard and working as a "millman".

In the 1871 Census of Canada Nelson, Elizabeth and their family were recorded as living in Lancaster. At the time of that census Nelson was working as a "millwright" at the Ritchie and Snowball Mill. The 1871 Lovell's Province of New Brunswick Directory also listed Nelson as employed as a "millwright" and living in Lancaster.

Elizabeth died tragically at age sixty on August 21, 1872. Following her daughter Phoebe Elizabeth, she was rushing to cross the train tracks to reach the platform at the Lancaster Station in South Bay, Saint John, New Brunswick, when she was hit by a PicNic Train as it was backing up into the station. Elizabeth was knocked 12 to 15 feet under the station platform suffering a fractured skull, from which she died soon after being hit. At the time of her death her husband Nelson was working at one of the Ritchie and Snowball mills in Miramichi, Northumberland, New Brunswick. He had just sent some money along with a letter to his wife which she was returning from picking up when her death occurred. A coroner's inquest was held two days later, on August 23, 1872, which concluded that her death was the result of a tragic accident. The exact location of Elizabeth's grave is not known at this time, but her death notice published on August 24, 1872 indicated she was to be interred in Carlton, Saint John, New Brunswick.

On January 6, 1873 Nelson, then age sixty-five, was married to his second wife Annie Sutherland, age twenty-seven, in Newcastle, Northumberland, New Brunswick by W. A. Coleman, a Baptist minister. Annie, who was living with her parents, James and Jane Sutherland in Richibucto, Kent, New Brunswick at that time, was born in Nova Scotia around 1846. The exact date and place of her birth have not been found.

When the McAlpine's Saint John Directory was prepared for 1874-1875, Nelson was listed as living in Fairville, Saint John, New Brunswick and still working as a "millwright".

It is believed that Nelson died sometime between the publishing of McAlpine's Saint John Directory in 1874 and his daughter Eliza Ann's death on September 21, 1882, when he was listed as deceased in her death notice. The exact date and cause of his death, as well as the location of his grave are unknown at this time.

Additional information regarding the life and death of Nelson's second wife Annie has also not been found.

SOURCES:

Nelson Williams
Birth: (1) Original Record of Maine Towns & Cities, Town of Bingham, Maine, Page 26, Picton Press, Rockland Maine 2005; (2) "Maine, Births and Christenings, 1739-1900," index, FamilySearch (https://familysearch.org/pal:/MM9.1.1/F4H9-WVZ).
Death:
Graveyard:

Elizabeth Dunham
Birth:
Marriage: (1) Saint John, New Brunswick, Marriage Registers, Book B, Page 535, Provincial Archives of New Brunswick; (2) Marriage Notice, "New Brunswick Vital Statistics from Newspapers", by Daniel F. Johnson, Volume 8 1839-1840, Number 320, Provincial Archives of New Brunswick.
Death: (1) Newspaper article, Saint John Daily Telegraph, August 22, 1872; (2) Death Notice, "New Brunswick Vital Statistics from Newspapers", by Daniel F. Johnson, Volume 32, Number 1006, Provincial Archives of New Brunswick.
Graveyard:

David D. Williams
Birth: Record of a Death, Maine Vital Records.
Death: Record of a Death, Maine Vital Records.
Graveyard: (1) "Moscow Union Cemetery" by Nancy Hamlin Davis and Ruth Hamlin, Record 593, Old Canada Road Historical Society; (2) Find A Grave Memorial # 8214990.

Annie Sutherland
Birth:
Marriage: (1) Northumberland, New Brunswick Marriage Registers, 1864-1887, Page 206; (2) Marriage Notice, "New Brunswick Vital Statistics from Newspapers", by Daniel F. Johnson, Volume 33, Number 1701, Provincial Archives of New Brunswick.
Death:
Graveyard:

Historical Accounts: (1) Williams/Briggs Family Bible, from the collection of Jeffrey N. Williams and Jacqueline Pon Williams; (2) 1830 United States Federal Census for Township No. 1, 4th Range, East Kennebec River, Somerset, Maine; (3) 1840 United States Federal Census for Township No. 1, 4th Range, East Kennebec River, Somerset, Maine, Page 94; (4) 1871 Census of Canada for Lancaster, Saint John, New Brunswick, Page 33; (5) 1871 Census of Canada for Richibucto, Kent, New Brunswick, Page 26; (6) Hutchinson's Saint John Directory 1863-1864, Page 258; (7) Lovell's Province of New Brunswick Directory for 1871, Page 230; (8) McAlpine's Saint John Directory 1874-1875, Page 361; (9) Death Notice for Mrs. Peter Cusack (Eliza Ann Williams), "New Brunswick Vital Statistics from Newspapers", by Daniel F. Johnson, Volume 58, Number 288, Provincial Archives of New Brunswick.

II

The Second Generation: The Children of Nelson Williams

II

The Second Generation:

The Children of Nelson Williams

John Nelson Williams

(1842 - 1924)

The first child of Nelson Williams and Elizabeth Dunham was John Nelson who was born on October 19, 1842 in Skowhegan, Somerset, Maine, USA.

On July 4, 1865 in Indiantown, Saint John, New Brunswick, Canada, John Nelson, age twenty-two, was married to Nancy Jane Coleman, age nineteen, of Portland, Saint John, New Brunswick by Reverend Edwin C. Cady Pastor of the Portland Baptist Church. Nancy Jane was born on April 1, 1846 in Portland to James B. Coleman and Jane Graves.

John Nelson and Nancy Jane had ten children together.

Silas B.	*b. 1867*	*d. May 7, 1887*
Caroline Louisa	b. November 14, 1868	d. January 6, 1923
Bessie D.	b. July 1, 1871	d. April 28, 1938
James Benjamin	b. August 17, 1873	d. February 25, 1946
Charles Grierson	b. 1876	d. October 15, 1909
Emma Lillian	b. May 31, 1878	d. April 27, 1939
Harry H.	b. January 18, 1881	d. July 8, 1902
Ewen McFarlane	b. August 26, 1883	d. January 18, 1965
Jennie Graves	b. October 21, 1886	d. October 27, 1936
Mary B.	b. June 4, 1890	d. October 27, 1963

Back Row: Ewen Williams, Mary Williams Gilbert and William Stout;
Front Row: Nancy Coleman Williams, John Nelson Williams and Jennie Williams Stout, circa 1907
(Photograph Courtesy of James Harold Williams and Helene Comeau Williams)

On August 20, 1869 John Nelson became the first lighthouse keeper for the newly established Swift Point Lighthouse in Green Head, Saint John, New Brunswick. He continued as the keeper of the lighthouse until 1886. John Nelson was paid $80.00 per year for his services maintaining the lighthouse.

Swift Point Lighthouse in 2012
(Photograph from the collection of Jeffrey N. Williams and Jacqueline Pon Williams)

In the 1871 and 1881 Census' of Canada John Nelson, Nancy Jane and their family were recorded as living in Lancaster, Saint John, New Brunswick. His occupation was listed as "lighthouse keeper". The 1871 Lovell's Province of New Brunswick Directory listed John Nelson as living in Green Head and working as a "laborer".

The first child of John Nelson and Nancy Jane, Silas B., died at the age of twenty-one on May 16, 1887of an unknown cause in Nelson, Northumberland, New Brunswick. No record has been found to indicate that he ever married or had any children. His funeral was held at 2:00 o'clock on Thursday May 19, 1887 at the home of his maternal grandfather, James B. Coleman, at the corner of Victoria and Metcalf Streets in Indiantown. The location of his burial is not known at this time.

When the 1891 and 1901 Census' of Canada were taken John Nelson, Nancy Jane and their children were still living in Lancaster. In the 1891 census John Nelson was recorded as working as a "quarry man" and in the 1901 census he was listed as working as a "millman".

On September 29, 1917, at age 71, Nancy Jane died at the home of her daughter Emma Lillian (Williams) Anderson located at 270 Guilford Street, Saint John West, Saint John, New Brunswick. The cause of her death was listed as "cerebral apoplexy". The funeral for Nancy Jane was held on Monday, October 1, 1918 at 2:00 P.M. and she was buried that same day in Lot 253, Grave 297 at the Old Cedar Hill Cemetery in Saint John West.

The 1921 Census of Canada recorded John Nelson as retired and living with his daughter Emma Lillian (Williams) Anderson and her family in Guys Ward, Saint John City, Saint John, New Brunswick.

John Nelson survived his wife by almost seven years, dying on March 22, 1924 at age eighty-one in Milford, Saint John, New Brunswick. His cause of death was listed as "uremia". The funeral for John Nelson was held at the home of his daughter Emma Lillian at 180 Rodney Street, Saint John West with Reverend C. R. Freeman performing the service. On March 24, 1924 John Nelson was buried in Saint John West at the Old Cedar Hill Cemetery in Lot 253, Grave 298.

Gravestones for John Nelson Williams (left) and Nancy Jane Coleman (right)
(Photographs from the collection of Jeffrey N. Williams and Jacqueline Pon Williams)

SOURCES:

John Nelson Williams
Birth: (1) Department of Health New Brunswick, Certificate of Registration of Death, Saint John City and County Sub-Health District; (2) 1901 Census of Canada, Lancaster, Saint John, New Brunswick, Page 21.
Death: (1) Department of Health New Brunswick, Certificate of Registration of Death, Saint John City and County Sub-Health District; (2) "New Brunswick Provincial Deaths 1815-1938," index, FamilySearch (https://familysearch.org/pal:MM9.1.1/XGZX-3D3); (3) Obituary, The Saint John Globe, March 24, 1924.
Graveyard: (1) Listing of Interments prepared by Greenwood Cedar Hill Cemetery Company, Saint John West, Saint John, New Brunswick, November 2012; (2) Department of Health New Brunswick, Certificate of Registration of Death, Saint John City and County Sub-Health District.

Nancy Jane Coleman
Birth: 1901 Census of Canada, Lancaster, Saint John, New Brunswick, Page 21.
Marriage: (1) Marriage Records 1865, Microfilm Roll RS156, Saint John Free Public Library, Saint John, New Brunswick; (2) Marriage Notice, "New Brunswick Vital Statistics from Newspapers", by Daniel F. Johnson, Volume 23, Number 2305, Provincial Archives of New Brunswick.
Death: (1) Deaths, Registration Division of Saint John City and County, New Brunswick; (2) Local Board of Heath, Return of a Death on Application for a Burial Permit, Volume A26, Page 813, City of Saint John, Provincial Archives of New Brunswick; (3) Obituary, The Daily Telegraph, Monday, October 1, 1917, Page 5.
Graveyard: (1) Listing of Interments prepared by Greenwood Cedar Hill Cemetery Company, Saint John West, Saint John, New Brunswick, November 2012; (2) Local Board of Heath, Return of a Death on Application for a Burial Permit, Volume A26, Page 813, City of Saint John, Provincial Archives of New Brunswick.

Silas B. Williams
Birth:
Death: (1) Death Notice, "New Brunswick Vital Statistics from Newspapers", by Daniel F. Johnson, Volume 67, Number 3660, Provincial Archives of New Brunswick; (2) Death Notice, "New Brunswick Vital Statistics from Newspapers", by Daniel F. Johnson, Volume 68, Number 695, Provincial Archives of New Brunswick.
Graveyard:

Historical Accounts: (1) 1871 Census of Canada, Lancaster, Saint John, New Brunswick, Page 28; (2) 1881 Census of Canada, Lancaster, Saint John, New Brunswick, Page 1; (3) 1891 Census of Canada, Lancaster, Saint John, New Brunswick, Page 113; (4) 1901 Census of Canada, Lancaster, Saint John, New Brunswick, Page 21; (5) 1921 Census of Canada, Saint John, Saint John, New Brunswick, Page 6; (6) Lighthousefriends.com – Swift Point Lighthouse; (7) Annual Report of the Department of Marines and Fisheries for the year ending June 30, 1870; (8) Lovell's Province of New Brunswick Directory for 1871, Page 213.

Silas M. Williams

(1847 - 1918)

Silas M., born in Richmond, Virginia, USA on July 15, 1847, was the third child of Nelson Williams and Elizabeth Dunham. (Although no record has been found to indicate that Silas M.'s parents ever lived for any period of time in Richmond, Virginia several documents, including the 1892 Marriage Register for Northumberland County, New Brunswick, Canada, the 1911 Census of Canada, a 1916 Immigration Memorandum and his obituary support his place of birth)

The 1871 Census of Canada recorded Silas M., age twenty-three, as living with his parents in Lancaster, Saint John, New Brunswick where he was working as a "millwright".

Sometime before 1880 Silas M. married Mary Ann Brown in the Province of New Brunswick, Canada. The exact place and date of their marriage are not known. Additionally Mary Ann's date and place of birth, as well as the names of her parents, have not been found. However from the published census records it is believed she was born around 1850.

During their marriage Silas M. and Mary Ann had three children together.

Percy B.	b. December 22, 1879	d. September 6, 1962
Bessie	b. January 20, 1882	d. May 18, 1939
Helen Gertrude	b. July 2, 1885	d. August 31, 1977

In the 1881 Census of Canada, Silas M., Mary Ann and their first child Percy B. were recorded as living in Nelson, Northumberland, New Brunswick. Silas M.'s occupation was listed as "millwright".

Sometime between 1885 and 1891 it is believed that Mary Ann died. The exact date and place of her death, as well as the place her burial are unknown.

When the 1891 Census of Canada was taken, Silas M., a widower, was still working as a "millwright" and living in Nelson with his three children.

On November 15, 1892, Silas M., then age forty-five, was married to his second wife thirty-three year old Elizabeth Flett at the St. Andrews Manse in Nelson by Reverend Joseph McCoy. Elizabeth, born in Nelson on August 22, 1857, was the daughter of James Flett and Catherine Leslie.

Silas M. and his second wife Elizabeth had two children together.

John James	b. October 26, 1893	d. April 23, 1915
Silas Leslie	b. October 24, 1898	d. November 4, 1970

The 1901 and 1911 Census' of Canada recorded Silas M., Elizabeth and their family as living in Nelson with Silas M. continuing to work as a "millwright".

In the early 1900's Silas M. was listed in the ledger of the South Nelson Road Brickyard and Store, which most likely indicates that during that time he either worked for the South Nelson Road Brickyard or traded his labor for bricks and goods from their store.

On December 25, 1916 Silas M. and Elizabeth crossed the Canada - United States border at Port Huron, St. Clair, Michigan on their way to visit Silas M.'s son from his first marriage, Percy B. Williams, in Oconto, Oconto, Wisconsin. In the Immigration Services "Primary Inspection Memorandum" Silas M. was described as being 5' 7½ " tall with a ruddy complexion, gray hair and blue eyes. In that same document Elizabeth was listed as being 5' 4" tall, with a dark complexion, gray hair and blue eyes.

Two years later, on December 24, 1918, Silas M. died at the age of seventy-one in Nelson. His cause of death was listed as "pneumonia". He was buried in the St. James United Cemetery in Nelson.

In the 1921 Census of Canada, Elizabeth was recorded as living with her son Silas Leslie in Nelson.

When the 1935 List of Electors for Northumberland County was published Elizabeth was recorded as a widow living on South Nelson Road in the Nelson area.

Elizabeth outlived her husband Silas M. by almost twenty years dying, at the age of eighty-one, of "apoplexy" on November 29, 1938 in South Nelson, Northumberland, New Brunswick. Her funeral was held on December 1, 1938 at her home with services conducted by Reverend M.C.P. Macintosh. Elizabeth is also buried in the St. James United Cemetery in Nelson.

SOURCES:

Silas M. Williams
Birth: Obituary, North Shore Leader, January 3, 1919.
Death: (1) Deaths, Registration Division of Northumberland County, New Brunswick; (2) Obituary, North Shore Leader, January 3, 1919.
Graveyard: "Cemeteries of the Parish of Nelson, Northumberland County, Province of New Brunswick, Canada", Page 55, NB Genealogical Society-Miramichi Branch, 2002.

Mary Ann Brown
Birth:
Marriage:
Death:
Graveyard:

Elizabeth Flett
Birth: Province of New Brunswick, Certificate of Registration of Death, Northumberland Sub-Health District.
Marriage: (1) Marriage, Registration Division of Northumberland County, New Brunswick; (2) Marriage Notice, "New Brunswick Vital Statistics from Newspapers", by Daniel F. Johnson, Volume 83, Number 1027, Provincial Archives of New Brunswick.
Death: (1) Province of New Brunswick, Certificate of Registration of Death, Northumberland Sub-Health District; (2) Obituary, Miramichi Branch, The New Brunswick Genealogical Society, Obituary Database.
Graveyard: "Cemeteries of the Parish of Nelson, Northumberland County, Province of New Brunswick, Canada", Page 55, NB Genealogical Society-Miramichi Branch, 2002.

Historical Accounts: (1) 1871 Census of Canada, Lancaster, Saint John, New Brunswick, Page 32; (2) 1881 Census of Canada, Nelson, Northumberland, New Brunswick, Page 52; (3) 1891 Census of Canada, Nelson, Northumberland, New Brunswick Page 29; (4) 1901 Census of Canada, Nelson, Northumberland, New Brunswick, Page 7; (5) 1911 Census of Canada, Nelson, Northumberland, New Brunswick, Page 15; (6) 1921 Census of Canada, Nelson, Northumberland, New Brunswick, Page 9; (7) Primary Inspection Memorandum, U.S. Department of Labor Immigration Services, 12/25/1916; (8) Michigan Passenger and Crew Lists, 1903-1965; (9) "Nelson and Its Neighbors, 300 Years on the Miramichi" , by Earl J. English, Page 106, Published by Walco Print & Litho Ltd., Chatham, New Brunswick, 1987; (10) List of Electors, 1935, Electoral District of Northumberland, N.B., Rural Polling Division No 39, Parish of Nelson, Page 2.

Eliza Ann Williams

(1849 - 1882)

The fourth child of Nelson Williams and Elizabeth Dunham, Eliza Ann, was born in 1849 in Somerset County, Maine, USA. The exact date and place of her birth has not been found.

Eliza Ann Williams, circa December 1872 (left) and Peter Cusack (right)
(Photographs Courtesy of Donald Emerson Smith and Donna Smith)

When the 1871 Census of Canada was taken, Eliza Ann then age twenty-two was recorded as living with her parents in Lancaster, Saint John, New Brunswick, Canada.

At age twenty-three Eliza Ann was married to Peter Cusack, age thirty, in South Bay, Saint John, New Brunswick on December 12, 1872 by Reverend H. P. Cowperwaite. Peter, born in 1842 in Millstream, Kings, New Brunswick was the son of James Cusack and Mary Jonah. The exact date of his birth has not been found.

Eliza Ann and Peter had five children.

Frederick Willard	b. September 15, 1873	d. October 16, 1956
George Clifford	b. July 31, 1874	d. April 3, 1953
Mary Alice	b. November 8, 1875	d. March 12, 1961
Minnie Loretta	b. October 15, 1877	d. January 14, 1968
Eliza Blanche	*b. February 21, 1879*	*d. December 13, 1879*

Eliza Blanche, the fifth child of Eliza Ann and Peter, died in South Bay at nine months twenty-one days old on December 13, 1879. The cause of her death and her place of burial are not known.

The 1881 Census of Canada recorded Eliza Ann, Peter and their children as living in Lancaster. Peter was listed as working as a "teamster".

On August 9, 1882 Eliza Ann, then age thirty-three, died in South Bay. Her death notice indicated that she died "after a lingering illness of three years". The exact nature of her illness and the location of her burial have not been found.

The McAlpine Directory for 1889 listed Peter as working in South Bay as a "teamster". By the time the 1891 Census of Canada was taken Peter was working as a "painter" and living with his children in Lancaster.

Peter died suddenly on July 4, 1894 in Douglas, Northumberland, New Brunswick. His obituary in The Gleaner said that he "took sick and died in fifteen minutes" at the Douglas Boom. His place of burial has not been found.

SOURCES:

Eliza Ann Williams
Birth:
Death: (1) Death Notice, Daily Sun, Thursday, September 21, 1882, Page 3; (2) Death Notice, "New Brunswick Vital Statistics from Newspapers", by Daniel F. Johnson, Volume 58, Number 288, Provincial Archives of New Brunswick.
Graveyard:

Peter Cusack
Birth:
Marriage: Marriage Notice, "New Brunswick Vital Statistics from Newspapers", by Daniel F. Johnson, Volume 32, Number 362, Provincial Archives of New Brunswick.
Death: Death Notice, "New Brunswick Vital Statistics from Newspapers", by Daniel F. Johnson, Volume 91, Number 1362, Provincial Archives of New Brunswick.
Graveyard:

Eliza Blanche Cusack
Birth:
Death: Death Notice, "New Brunswick Vital Statistics from Newspapers", by Daniel F. Johnson, Volume 47, Number 1189, Provincial Archives of New Brunswick.
Graveyard:

Historical Accounts: (1) 1871 Census of Canada, Lancaster, Saint John, New Brunswick, Page 32; (2) 1881 Census of Canada, Lancaster, Saint John, New Brunswick, Page 24; (3) 1891 Census of Canada, Lancaster, Saint John, New Brunswick, Page 24; (4) 1889 McAlpine's Directory for New Brunswick, Page 890; (5) Genealogy Notes for Eliza Ann Williams, Peter Cusack and their children provided by Donald Emerson Smith and Donna Smith.

Phoebe Elizabeth Williams

(1852 - 1915)

Phoebe Elizabeth was the fifth child of Nelson Williams and Elizabeth Dunham. Born in Oak Point, Kings, New Brunswick on September 24, 1852, she was the first child of Nelson and Elizabeth to be born in Canada.

Phoebe Elizabeth Williams, circa December 1872
(Photographs Courtesy of Donald Emerson Smith and Donna Smith)

In the 1871 Census of Canada Phoebe Elizabeth, age eighteen, was recorded as living with her parents in Lancaster, Saint John, New Brunswick.

On August 23, 1872, Phoebe Elizabeth appeared as a witness at the Coroner's inquest into the accidental death of her mother who was hit by a train at the Lancaster Station in South Bay, Saint John, New Brunswick.

At the age of twenty, on July 1, 1873, Phoebe Elizabeth was married to Wilford Welling Betts age twenty-three in Saint John County, New Brunswick. The exact location of their wedding is not known. Wilford Welling, born on August 9, 1849 in Shediac, Westmoreland, New Brunswick, was the son of Henry Betts and Eleanor Cusack.

Phoebe Elizabeth and Wilford Welling had seven children together.

Arthur Welling	b. November 6, 1873	d. September 3, 1953
John Wilford Hartley	b. May 10, 1875	d. March 6, 1950
Adelaide Winnifred	b. February 1878	d. December 5, 1901
Frederick Nelson	*b. March 27, 1881*	*d. March 29, 1881*
Percival N. H.	b. December 14, 1882	d. November 10, 1962
Charles Clinton	b. October 13, 1885	d. September 28, 1949
Florence Eveline	*b. August 30, 1889*	*d. May 6, 1892*

The fourth child of Phoebe Elizabeth and Wilford Welling, Frederick Nelson, was two days old when he died in Green Head, Saint John, New Brunswick on March 29, 1881. The cause of his death and the place of his burial have not been found.

The 1881 and 1891Census' of Canada recorded Phoebe Elizabeth, Wilford Welling and their children living in Lancaster. In the 1881 census Wilford Welling was listed as working as a "blacksmith". At the time of the 1891 census Wilford Welling had changed occupations and was working as a "sawmill man".

Florence Eveline, the seventh child of Phoebe Elizabeth and Wilford Welling, was two years eight months old when she died of "diphtheria" at the family home in Lancaster on May 6, 1892. Her place of burial is not known.

In the 1901 and 1911 Census' of Canada Phoebe Elizabeth, Wilford Welling and their family were still living in Lancaster where Wilford Welling was working as a "carpenter".

Phoebe Elizabeth died at the age of sixty-three on December 1, 1915 in Fairville, Saint John, New Brunswick. Her cause of death was recorded as "pneumonia". She was buried in Lot 46, Avenue E at St. George's Cemetery in Saint John West, Saint John, New Brunswick.

Sometime after the death of his first wife Wilford Welling was married to Emeline (also known as Emma) Thomas. The exact date and place, as well as the name of the presiding official, have not been found. Emeline Thomas, the daughter of Benjamin Thomas and Hannah Gough, was born on October 18, 1858 in Saint John West. No record has been found indicating that Wilford Welling and Emeline had any children during their marriage.

Emeline died on March 11, 1920 at the family home at 30 George Street in Fairville at the age of sixty-one. Her cause of death was listed as "acute cardiac failure". She was buried in the Church of Good Shepherd Cemetery in Saint John West.

When the 1921 Census of Canada was taken, Wilford Welling was recorded as still living on George Street in Fairville with his son Charles Clinton. In that census Wilford Welling was listed as working as a "laborer".

On July 9, 1923 Wilford Welling, then age seventy-four, was married to his third wife the widow Elizabeth (Buchanan) Gregg, age sixty, in Fairville. Elizabeth, born around 1857-1863 in Saint John West, was the daughter of Samuel Buchanan and Catherine Gardener. Wilford Welling and Elizabeth did not have any children during their marriage.

Wilford Welling died at his home located at 27 Lancaster Street, Saint John West on March 20, 1932 at the age of eighty-two. His cause of death was listed as "chronic nephritis". He too was buried in Lot 46, Avenue E at St. George's Cemetery in Saint John West.

The third wife of Wilford Welling, Elizabeth, was married for the third time to William Henry Hanson in 1934. She died of "carcinoma of the cervix" on July 21, 1936 at the Saint John General Hospital in Saint John City, Saint John, New Brunswick. Her place of burial is not known.

Betts Family Plot Marker, St. George's Cemetery, Saint John West
(Photograph from the collection of Jeffrey N. Williams and Jacqueline Pon Williams)

Headstones for Phoebe Elizabeth Williams (left) and Wilford Welling Betts (right)
(Photographs from the collection of Jeffrey N. Williams and Jacqueline Pon Williams)

SOURCES:

Phoebe Elizabeth Williams
Birth: (1) Deaths, Registration Division of Saint John City and County, New Brunswick; (2) 1901 Census of Canada, Lancaster, Saint John, New Brunswick, Page 32.
Death: (1) Deaths, Registration Division of Saint John City and County, New Brunswick; (2) Obituary, Saint John Globe, Thursday, December 20, 1915, Page 2.
Graveyard: (1) Listing of Interments prepared by Greenwood Cedar Hill Cemetery Company, Saint John West, Saint John, New Brunswick, November 2012; (2) Find A Grave Memorial #74421494.

Wilford Welling Betts
Birth: (1) Department of Health - New Brunswick, Certificate of Registration of Death, Saint John City and County Sub-Health District 1901; (2) 1901 Census of Canada, Lancaster, Saint John, New Brunswick, Page 32.
Marriage:
Death: Department of Health - New Brunswick, Certificate of Registration of Death, Saint John City and County Sub-Health District.
Graveyard: Listing of Interments prepared by Greenwood Cedar Hill Cemetery Company, Saint John West, Saint John, New Brunswick, November 2012; (2) Find A Grave Memorial #74421565.

Frederick Nelson Betts
Birth: Death Notice, "New Brunswick Vital Statistics from Newspapers", by Daniel F. Johnson, Volume 54, Number 2523, Provincial Archives of New Brunswick.
Death: Death Notice, "New Brunswick Vital Statistics from Newspapers", by Daniel F. Johnson, Volume 54, Number 2523, Provincial Archives of New Brunswick.
Graveyard:

Florence Eveline Betts
Birth: Births, Registration Division of Saint John City and County, New Brunswick.
Death: (1) Deaths, Return of Clergyman, Occupier or Other Person, Registration Division of Saint John City and County, New Brunswick; (2) Death Notice, "New Brunswick Vital Statistics from Newspapers", by Daniel F. Johnson, Volume 85, Number 1291, Provincial Archives of New Brunswick.
Graveyard:

Emeline Thomas
Birth: Department of Health - New Brunswick, Certificate of Registration of Death, Saint John City and County Sub-Health District.
Death: (1) Department of Health - New Brunswick, Certificate of Registration of Death, Saint John City and County Sub-Health District; (2) Obituary, Saint John Globe, Friday, March 12, 1920, Page 2.
Graveyard:

Elizabeth Buchanan Gregg
Birth:
Marriage: Province of New Brunswick, Department of Health, Official Notice of Marriage, Saint John City and County Sub-Health District.
Death: Province of New Brunswick - Certificate of Registration of Death, Saint John City and County Sub-Health District.
Graveyard:

Historical Accounts: (1) 1881 Census of Canada, Lancaster, Saint John, New Brunswick; (2) 1891 Census of Canada, Lancaster, Saint John, New Brunswick, Page 112; (3) 1901 Census of Canada, Lancaster, Saint John, New Brunswick, Page 32; (4) 1911 Census of Canada, Lancaster, Saint John, New Brunswick, Page 23; (5) 1921 Census of Canada, Lancaster, Saint John, New Brunswick, Page 13; (6) Death Notice, "New Brunswick Vital Statistics from Newspapers", by Daniel F. Johnson, Volume 32, Number 1006, Provincial Archives of New Brunswick.

Benjamin Franklin Williams

(1855 - 1938)

The sixth child of Nelson Williams and Elizabeth Dunham was Benjamin Franklin. He was born on August 24, 1855 in Northumberland County, New Brunswick, Canada. The exact location of his birth is not known.

The 1871 Census of Canada recorded Benjamin Franklin, age fifteen, as living with his parents in Lancaster, Saint John, New Brunswick.

On July 17, 1877 in Newcastle, Northumberland, New Brunswick, Benjamin Franklin, age twenty-one, was married to Jane Brown, also age twenty-one, by Reverend T. M. Monroe, Pastor of the Newcastle Baptist Church. Jane, born on October 20, 1855 in St. Martins, Saint John, New Brunswick, was the daughter of Isaiah F. Brown and Caroline Bradshaw. Benjamin Franklin's brother Silas M. Williams and his wife Mary Ann Brown served as witnesses to the marriage.

Benjamin Franklin and Jane had seven children together.

James Franklin	b. September 5, 1877	d. July 13, 1935
Olive Edna	b. October 30, 1879	d. March 21, 1951
John Garnett	b. May 20, 1882	d. February 17, 1937
Estella	b. September 7, 1884	d. November 27, 1973
Edith May	b. May 23, 1887	d. August 22, 1963
Charles Seeley	b. June 24, 1890	d. December 18, 1960
Frederick John	b. September 18, 1894	d. January 10, 1955

In the 1881, 1891, 1901, 1911 and 1921 Census' of Canada, Benjamin Franklin, Jane and their family were recorded as living in Lancaster, Saint John, New Brunswick. In 1891 Benjamin Franklin was listed as working as a "quarryman", in the 1901 census as a "mill man" and in both 1911 and 1921 censuses as a "laborer".

Benjamin Franklin died at the age of eighty-three on December 5, 1938 in the Saint John General Hospital in Saint John City, Saint John, New Brunswick. His cause of death was listed as "chronic degenerative heart disease". At the time of his death he and his wife Jane were living at 39 Havelock Street in Saint John West, Saint John, New Brunswick.

The funeral for Benjamin Franklin was held at 2:30 P.M. on Thursday, December 8th at 206 Ludlow Street, Saint John West, at the home of his son Charles Seeley. He was buried in his family plot, Lot 295, Avenue 49, at the Old Cedar Hill Cemetery in Saint John West.

Jane died a little over four months later on April 17, 1939 at the home of her son Charles Seeley at 206 Ludlow Street in Saint John West when she was also age eighty-three. Her cause of death was listed as "pneumonia". She too was buried in the Benjamin Franklin Williams family plot, Lot 295, Avenue 49, at the Old Cedar Hill Cemetery in Saint John.

Headstone for Benjamin Franklin Williams
(Photograph from the collection of Jeffrey N. Williams and Jacqueline Pon Williams)

It should be noted here that the Benjamin Franklin Williams family plot at the Old Cedar Hill Cemetery in Saint John West contained only single a marker for B. Williams when it was visited in October 2012 and October 2016.

SOURCES:

Benjamin Franklin Williams
Birth: (1) Province of New Brunswick - Certificate of Registration of Death, Saint John City and County Sub-Health District; (2) 1901 Census of Canada, Lancaster, Saint John, New Brunswick, Page 10.
Death: (1) Province of New Brunswick - Certificate of Registration of Death, Saint John City and County Sub-Health District; (2) Obituary & Death Notice, Evening Times Globe, Saturday, Wednesday, December 7, 1938, Page 11; (3) Brenan's Funeral Home Records, Saint John - Provincial Archives of New Brunswick.
Graveyard: (1) Listing of Interments prepared by Greenwood Cedar Hill Cemetery Company, Saint John West, Saint John, New Brunswick, November 2012; (2) Brenan's Funeral Home Records, Saint John - Provincial Archives of New Brunswick.

Jane Brown
Birth: Province of New Brunswick - Certificate of Registration of Death, Saint John City and County Sub-Health District.
Marriage: (1) "New Brunswick Marriage Registers, 1789-1889",images, FamilySearch (https//familysearch.org/pal:/MM9.3.1/TH-1971-27455-260-27?cc=2001063); (2) Marriage Notice, "New Brunswick Vital Statistics from Newspapers", by Daniel F. Johnson, Volume 41, #458, Provincial Archives of New Brunswick.
Death: Province of New Brunswick - Certificate of Registration of Death, Saint John City and County Sub-Health District.
Graveyard: Listing of Interments prepared by Greenwood Cedar Hill Cemetery Company, Saint John West, Saint John, New Brunswick, November 2012.

Historical Accounts: (1) 1871 Census of Canada, Lancaster, Saint John, New Brunswick, Page 33; (2) 1871 Census of Canada, St. Martins, Saint John, New Brunswick, Page 2; (3) 1881 Census of Canada, Lancaster, Saint John, New Brunswick, Page 2; (4) 1891 Census of Canada, Lancaster, Saint John, New Brunswick, Page 21; (5) 1901 Census of Canada, Lancaster, Saint John, New Brunswick, Page 10; (6) 1911 Census of Canada, Lancaster, Saint John, New Brunswick, Page 23; (7) 1921 Census of Canada, Lancaster, Saint John, New Brunswick, Page 23.

III

The Third Generation:

The Grand Children of Nelson Williams

The Children of John Nelson Williams

The Children of Silas M. Williams

The Children of Eliza Ann Williams

The Children of Phoebe Elizabeth Williams

The Children of Benjamin Franklin Williams

Caroline Louisa Williams

(1868 - 1923)

The second child of John Nelson Williams and Nancy Jane Coleman was Caroline Louisa (commonly known as Carrie). She was born in Randolph, Saint John, New Brunswick, Canada on November 14, 1868.

At age twenty-one, on June 19, 1890, Caroline Louisa was married to James Burley Pollock, age thirty-seven, at her father's house in Randolph by Reverend C. H. Martell, a Baptist minister. James Burley was born on March 30, 1853 in Portland, Saint John, New Brunswick to John and Margaret Pollock. At the time of his marriage to Caroline Louisa, James Burley was working as a "mason".

Shortly after their marriage, the 1891 Census of Canada recorded Caroline Louisa and James Burley as living in Guy's Ward, Saint John, New Brunswick.

Caroline Louisa and James Burley had nine children together.

John	*b. July 1891*	*d. December 9, 1892*
Nancy Jane	*b. June 1893*	*d. July 21, 1893*
James Clarence	b. October 20, 1894	d.
Ralph Gordon	b. January 8, 1897	d. June 14, 1953
Ada Olive	b. November 2, 1898	d. April 23, 1932
Arthur Edward	*b. April 2, 1901*	*d. August 3, 1922*
Caroline Louisa	b. August 11, 1903	d. February 15, 1937
Emma Lillian	*b. July 29, 1906*	*d. June 27, 1907*
Grace Doris	*b. August 8, 1911*	*d.*

On December 9, 1892 the first child of Caroline Louisa and James Burley, John, died at the family home on Winslow Street in Carlton, Saint John, New Brunswick at the age of one year and five months. The cause of his death was recorded as "diphtheria". He was buried in the James Burley Pollock family plot Lot 162, Avenue N, at the Old Cedar Hill Cemetery in Saint John West, Saint John, New Brunswick.

A little over seven months later, on July 21, 1893 Nancy Jean, the second child of Caroline Louisa and James Burley, died of "inflammation of the bowels" at the family home on Winslow Street in Carlton. She was just three weeks old at the time of her death. Nancy Jean was also buried in the family plot, Lot 162, Avenue N, at the Old Cedar Hill Cemetery in Saint John West.

The 1901 Census of Canada recorded Caroline Louisa, James Burley and their children as living Guy's Ward where James was working as a "mason".

Emma Lillian, the seventh child of Caroline Louisa and James Burley, died at the age of ten months twenty eight days old of "bronchopneumonia" at the family home at 261 Guilford Street in Saint John West on June 27, 1907. She was also buried in the James Burley Pollock family plot, Lot 162, Avenue N, at the Old Cedar Hill Cemetery in Saint John West.

In the 1911 Census of Canada, Caroline Louisa, James Burley and their family were recorded as still living at 261 Guilford Street in Saint John West.

James Burley died at the family home at 21 Champlain Street in Saint John West on January 20, 1917. The exact cause of James Burley's death is not known at this time. His funeral was held at his residence on Tuesday January 23, 1917. James Burley was buried at the Old Cedar Hill Cemetery in Saint John West in his family plot on Avenue N, Lot 162.

When the 1921 Census of Canada was taken Caroline Louisa and her son Arthur Edward were still living at the family home on Champlain Street in Saint John West. Arthur Edward was listed as working as a "laborer" in that census.

Arthur Edward, the sixth child of Caroline Louisa and James Burley, died at the age of twenty-one on August 3, 1922 of "pulmonary tuberculosis" at the East Saint John Hospital, East Saint John, Saint John, New Brunswick. No record has been found to indicate that Arthur Edward ever married or had children. Like his father and his siblings he was buried in Avenue N, Lot 162 the James Burley Pollock family plot at the Old Cedar Hill Cemetery in Saint John West.

Almost five months later, on January 6, 1923 at the age of fifty-four, Caroline Louisa also died of "pulmonary tuberculosis" in the Saint John County Hospital in Saint John City, Saint John, New Brunswick. At the time of her death she was still living at 21 Champlain Street in Saint John West. Caroline Louisa was buried in the James Burley Pollock family plot alongside the rest of her family at the Old Cedar Hill Cemetery in Saint John West.

Additional information regarding the life and death of Grace Doris, the ninth child of Caroline Louisa and James Burley, has not been found. However it is known that she was not listed as living with her mother when the 1921 Census of Canada was taken and that she is buried in the family plot Lot 162, Avenue N, at the Old Cedar Hill Cemetery in Saint John West. As such her documented family history will end here.

It should be noted that the James Burley Pollock family plot at the Old Cedar Hill Cemetery in Saint John West contained no stones or markers when it was visited in October 2016.

SOURCES:

Caroline Louisa Williams
Birth: Department of Health New Brunswick, Certificate of Registration of Death, Saint John City and County Sub-Health District.
Death: Department of Health New Brunswick, Certificate of Registration of Death, Saint John City and County Sub-Health District.
Graveyard: (1) Listing of Interments prepared by Greenwood Cedar Hill Cemetery Company, Saint John West, Saint John, New Brunswick, September 2016; (2) Department of Health New Brunswick, Certificate of Registration of Death, Saint John City and County Sub-Health District.

James Burley Pollock
Birth: 1901 Census of Canada, Guy's Ward, Saint John, New Brunswick, Page 7.
Marriage: (1) Marriage, Registration Division of Saint John County, New Brunswick; (2) Acadia, Canada, Vital and Church Records (Drouin Collection), 1888-1895, Schedule B – Marriages, Page 33; (3) Marriage Notice, "New Brunswick Vital Statistics from Newspapers", by Daniel F. Johnson, Volume 77, Number 1639, Provincial Archives of New Brunswick.
Death: Obituary, Daily Telegraph, Tuesday, January 23, 1917, Page 5.
Graveyard: Listing of Interments prepared by Greenwood Cedar Hill Cemetery Company, Saint John West, Saint John, New Brunswick, September 2016.

John Pollock
Birth: Deaths, Registration Division of Saint John City and County, New Brunswick.
Death: (1) Deaths, Registration Division of Saint John City and County, New Brunswick; (2) "New Brunswick, Saint John, Saint John, Burial Permits, 1889-1919," database with images, FamilySearch (https://familysearch .org/ark:/61903/1:1:Q2WK-LCXF).
Graveyard: (1) Listing of Interments prepared by Greenwood Cedar Hill Cemetery Company, Saint John West, Saint John, New Brunswick, September 2016; (2) "New Brunswick, Saint John, Saint John, Burial Permits, 1889-1919," database with images, FamilySearch (https://familysearch.org/ark:/61903/1:1:Q2WK-LCXF).

Nancy Jean Pollock
Birth: Deaths, Registration Division of St. John City and County, New Brunswick.
Death: (1) Deaths, Registration Division of Saint John City and County, New Brunswick; (2) "New Brunswick, Saint John, Saint John, Burial Permits, 1889-1919," database with images, FamilySearch (https://familysearch .org/ark:/61903/1:1:Q2WK-LZJS).
Graveyard: (1) Listing of Interments prepared by Greenwood Cedar Hill Cemetery Company, Saint John West, Saint John, New Brunswick, September 2016; (2) "New Brunswick, Saint John, Saint John, Burial Permits, 1889-1919," database with images, FamilySearch (https://familysearch.org/ark:/61903/1:1:Q2WK-LZJS).

Emma Lillian Pollock
Birth: Births, Registration Division of Saint John County, New Brunswick.
Death: (1) Deaths, Registration Division of Saint John City and County, New Brunswick; (2) "New Brunswick, Saint John, Saint John, Burial Permits, 1889-1919," database with images, FamilySearch (https://familysearch .org/ark:/61903/1:1:Q2WK-G4NA).
Graveyard: (1) Listing of Interments prepared by Greenwood Cedar Hill Cemetery Company, Saint John West, Saint John, New Brunswick, September 2016; (2) "New Brunswick, Saint John, Saint John, Burial Permits, 1889-1919," database with images, FamilySearch (https://familysearch.org/ark:/61903/1:1:Q2WK-G4NA).

Arthur Edward Pollock
Birth: (1) Index to Late Registration of Births: County Series, Microfilm F18796, Provincial Archives of New Brunswick; (2) Department of Health New Brunswick, Certificate of Registration of Death, Saint John City and County Sub-Health District.
Death: Department of Health New Brunswick, Certificate of Registration of Death, Saint John City and County Sub-Health District.
Graveyard: Listing of Interments prepared by Greenwood Cedar Hill Cemetery Company, Saint John West, Saint John, New Brunswick, September 2016.

Grace Doris Pollock
Birth: Births, Registration Division of Saint John County, New Brunswick.
Death:
Graveyard: Listing of Interments prepared by Greenwood Cedar Hill Cemetery Company, Saint John West, Saint John, New Brunswick, September 2016.

Historical Accounts: (1) 1891 Census of Canada, Guy's Ward, Saint John, New Brunswick, Page 43; (2) 1901 Census of Canada, Guy's Ward, Saint John, New Brunswick, Page 7; (3) 1911 Census of Canada, Guy's Ward, Saint John, New Brunswick, Page 76; (4) 1921 Census of Canada, Guy's Ward, Saint John, New Brunswick, Pages 16 & 17.

Bessie D. Williams

(1871 - 1938)

Bessie D. was the third child of John Nelson Williams and Nancy Jane Coleman. She was born in Green Head, Saint John, New Brunswick, Canada on July 1, 1871.

At age twenty, on December 1, 1891, Bessie D. was married to Malcolm Campbell Golding, also age twenty, at the Baptist Parsonage in Carlton, Saint John, New Brunswick by Reverend J. A. Ford. Bessie D.'s brother Charles Grierson Williams was the listed witness to the wedding. Malcolm Campbell was born in The Narrows, Queens, New Brunswick on September 25, 1871 to George and Lydia Golding. At the time of his marriage to Bessie D., Malcolm Campbell was working as a "laborer"

Bessie D. and Malcolm Campbell had six children together.

Silas Boswell	b. December 31, 1891	d. September 11, 1942
Harry	*b. August 1, 1893*	*d. October 13, 1893*
Wallace C.	*b. April 30, 1895*	*d. May 21, 1895*
Bessie Evelyn	b. July 21, 1904	d. May 19, 1982
Percy N.	b. December 25, 1907	d. August 1, 1974
Harold Edgar	b. January 7, 1917	d. October 1, 1989

Two of Bessie D. and Malcolm Campbell's sons died at young ages at the family home in Randolph, Saint John, New Brunswick. Harry died on October 13, 1893 of "influenza" (also called "La Grippe") at the age of two months and Wallace C. died at twenty-one days old on May 21, 1895, his cause of death being listed as "sick since birth". The location of both their graves is unknown at this time.

In the 1901 Census of Canada, Bessie D., Malcolm Campbell and their son Silas Boswell were recorded as living in Lancaster, Saint John, New Brunswick. In that census Malcolm Campbell's occupation was recorded as a "millman".

According to the1910 United States Federal Census, Bessie D., Malcolm Campbell and three of their children immigrated to the United States in 1909. Upon their arrival they moved to Madison, Somerset, Maine where they were recorded as living in both the 1910 and 1920 United States Federal Census'. Malcolm Campbell was working as a "paper maker" at the time of both of those censuses.

On April 15, 1930, when the 1930 United States Federal Census was taken for Madison, Bessie D. and Malcolm Campbell were recorded as living at 7 Gray Street, which was next door to her brother Ewen McFarlane Williams and his wife Perla C. Garrick; and around the block from their son, Silas Boswell Campbell, and his family.

Malcolm Campbell and his daughter Bessie Evelyn were recorded as crossing the border by automobile into Calais, Washington, Maine on July 11, 1930 after visiting his uncle in Sussex, Kings New Brunswick. In the manifest documenting their crossing, Malcolm Campbell was described as being 5' 5" tall, with a fair complexion, gray hair and hazel eyes.

Bessie D. died at the age of sixty-six on April 28, 1938 in Madison. Her cause of death was recorded as “coronary occlusion”. Her funeral, which was conducted by Reverend Robie M. Brown, was held on Sunday May 1, 1938 at the home of her daughter, Bessie Evelyn (Golding) Moody, on Weston Avenue in Madison. Bessie D. was buried in Lot 709 at the Forest Hill Cemetery in Madison.

When the 1940 United States Federal Census was taken Malcolm Campbell was living with his daughter Bessie Evelyn and her husband Linwood G. Moody on West Mills Road in Anson, Somerset, Maine. In that census, as well as on his State of Maine Alien Registration Form dated June 28, 1940, Malcolm Campbell was recorded as working as a “cutter” for the Great Northern Paper Company at their local paper mill.

Outliving his wife by more than eighteen years, Malcolm Campbell died at the age of eighty-four on November 5, 1956 in South Berwick, York, Maine. His cause of death was listed as “hypertensive heart disease”. He too was buried in Lot 709 at the Forest Hill Cemetery in Madison.

SOURCES:

Bessie D. Williams
Birth: 1901 Census of Canada, Parish of Lancaster, Saint John, New Brunswick, Page 21.
Death: (1) Vital Records, Town of Madison Maine; (2) Funeral Notice, Lewiston Evening Journal, Lewiston, Maine, Monday May 2, 1938, Page 2.
Graveyard: (1) Records for Forest Hill Cemetery managed by the Town of Madison Maine; (2) “Forest Hill Cemetery”, updated by Dassie Jackson and Lena Arno in 2002 and 2003, page 57, Madison Historical Society, Madison, Maine.

Malcolm Campbell Golding
Birth: "Alien Registration- Golding, Malcolm C. (Anson, Somerset County)" (1940), Registrations, Book 7964, http://digitalmaine.com/alien_docs/7964.
Marriage: (1) Marriage, Registration Division of Saint John City and County, New Brunswick; (2) Acadia, Canada, Vital and Church Records (Drouin Collection), 1888-1895, Schedule B – Marriages, Page 55; (3) Marriage Notice, “New Brunswick Vital Statistics from Newspapers”, by Daniel F. Johnson, Volume 80, Number 1626, Provincial Archives of New Brunswick.
Death: Vital Records, Town of Madison Maine.
Graveyard: (1) Records for Forest Hill Cemetery managed by the Town of Madison Maine; (2) “Forest Hill Cemetery”, updated by Dassie Jackson and Lena Arno in 2002 and 2003, page 57, Madison Historical Society.

Harry Golding
Birth: Births, Registration Division of Saint John City and County, New Brunswick.
Death: Deaths, Registration Division of Saint John City and County, New Brunswick.
Graveyard:

Wallace C. Golding
Birth: (1) Births, Registration Division of Saint John City and County, New Brunswick; (2) Index to County Birth Registers, Microfilm F23160, Provincial Archives of New Brunswick
Death: Deaths, Registration Division of Saint John City and County, New Brunswick.
Graveyard:

Historical Accounts: (1) 1901 Census of Canada, Parish of Lancaster, Saint John, New Brunswick, Page 21; (2) 1910 United States Federal Census for Madison, Somerset, Maine, Page 19A; (3) 1920 United States Federal Census for Madison, Somerset, Maine, Page 2B; (4) 1930 United States Federal Census for Madison, Somerset, Maine, Page 10A; (5) 1940 United States Federal Census for Anson, Somerset, Maine, Page 13A; (6) U.S., Border Crossings from Canada to U.S., 1895-1956 [database on-line]. Provo, UT, USA: Ancestry.com Operations, Inc., 2010.

James Benjamin Williams

(1873 - 1946)

The fourth child of John Nelson Williams and Nancy Jane Coleman was James Benjamin. He was born on August 17, 1873 in Fairville, Saint John, New Brunswick, Canada.

James Benjamin, who at age twenty-one was working in the "milling industry", married Laura S. Nice age twenty-two at the Methodist Parsonage in Carleton, Saint John, New Brunswick. Reverend Charles H. Paisley was the officiant of their ceremony which was held on December 11, 1894. Laura S., the daughter of George Nice and Albenia Holland, was born on July 19, 1872 in Lancaster, Saint John, New Brunswick.

James Benjamin Williams and Laura S. Nice
(Photographs Courtesy of James H. Williams and Helene Comeau Williams)

James Benjamin and Laura S. had four children during their marriage.

Harold Edgar	b. July 25, 1895	d. October 29, 1953
Roy Nelson	*b. March 25, 1897*	*d. March 9, 1901*
Glendon Leslie	b. April 16, 1898	d. October 12, 1968
Edna Albina	b. June 12, 1900	d.

The 1901 Census of Canada recorded James Benjamin, Laura S. and their family as living in Lancaster. James Benjamin's occupation was listed as "teamster".

On March 9, 1901, after the 1901 Census of Canada was taken, Roy Nelson, the second child of James Benjamin and Laura S., died at the family home in Randolph, Saint John, New Brunswick just twenty-four days shy of his fourth birthday. The cause of his death was listed as “meningitis”. Roy Nelson’s place of his burial is not known.

Laura S., at age thirty-five, died at home in Randolph of “consumption” on December 3, 1907. She was buried in the Old Cedar Hill Cemetery in Saint John West, Saint John, New Brunswick in Lot 1061A, Grave 2.

Headstone for Laura Nice Williams
(Photograph from the collection of Jeffrey N. Williams and Jacqueline Pon Williams)

After his first wife’s death James Benjamin, married his second wife, Jennie Gertrude Brown. The exact date and place of their marriage has not been found. Jennie Gertrude, born on January 20, 1888 in Yarmouth, Nova Scotia, Canada, was the daughter of Andrew C. Brown and Mary D. Cripps.

Jennie Gertrude Brown
(Photograph Courtesy of James H. Williams and Helene Comeau Williams)

James Benjamin had five more children with his second wife Jennie Gertrude.

James Murray	b. September 10, 1910	d. October 7, 1987
Verna Jean	b. February 5, 1913	d. May 13, 2002
Robert Brown	b. January 15, 1915	d. June 22, 1983
Edwin John	b. December 20, 1917	d. January 10, 1980
George Royden	b. April 29, 1922	d. April 16, 2014

When the 1911 and 1921 Census' of Canada were taken, James Benjamin, his second wife Jennie Gertrude and their family were recorded as living in Lancaster with James Benjamin working at a "lime quarry".

On April 14, 1939, Jennie Gertrude died at age fifty-one of a "pelvic carcinoma" at home in Randolph. Her funeral was held at the home of her step-son Harold Edger Williams at 112 Victoria Street, Saint John City, Saint John, New Brunswick on Sunday April 16 at 3:30 P.M. Reverend W. U. Hatfield officiated and was assisted by Reverend Dr. S. S. Poole, Minister of the Germain Street Baptist Church. Jennie Gertrude was buried at the Cedar Hill Extension Cemetery in Saint John West in Section D, Lot 11, Grave 3.

In the 1940 Rural List of Electors for Lancaster, Rural Polling Division No. 146B, James Benjamin, a "foreman", and his two sons Robert Brown, a "laborer", and Edwin John, also a "laborer", were listed as being from Randolph.

On February 25, 1946, almost seven years after the death of his second wife, James Benjamin died at the age of seventy-two at the residence of Douglas Hamilton, 113 Bridge Street in Saint John City. His cause of death was listed as "colon cancer". During his lifetime James Benjamin had also worked in the Saint John area as a "machine shop engineer" and was a member of the Teamsters Union. James Benjamin's funeral was held at 2:00 P.M. at Brenan's Funeral Home, 111 Paradise Row, Saint John City on Wednesday February 27, 1946. He was buried at the Cedar Hill Cemetery Extension in Saint John West alongside his second wife, in Section D, Lot 11, Grave 1.

Gravestone for James Benjamin Williams and Jennie Brown Williams
(Photograph from the collection of Jeffrey N. Williams and Jacqueline Pon Williams)

SOURCES:

James Benjamin Williams
Birth: Province of New Brunswick, Certificate of Registration of Death, Saint John City and County Sub-Health District.
Death: (1) Province of New Brunswick, Certificate of Registration of Death, Saint John City and County Sub-Health District; (2) Obituary, from the collection of James H. Williams and Helene Comeau Williams.
Graveyard: Listing of Interments prepared by Greenwood Cedar Hill Cemetery Company, Saint John West, Saint John, New Brunswick, November 2012.

Laura S. Nice
Birth: 1901 Census of Canada, Lancaster, Saint John, New Brunswick, Page 20.
Marriage: (1) Marriage, Registration Division of Saint John City and County, New Brunswick; (2) Acadia, Canada, Vital and Church Records (Drouin Collection), 1888-1895, Schedule B – Marriages, Page 79; (3) Marriage Notice, "New Brunswick Vital Statistics from Newspapers", by Daniel F. Johnson, Volume 95, Number 1117, Provincial Archives of New Brunswick.
Death: Deaths, Registration Division of Saint John City and County, New Brunswick.
Graveyard: Listing of Interments prepared by Greenwood Cedar Hill Cemetery Company, Saint John West, Saint John, New Brunswick, November 2012.

Roy Nelson Williams
Birth: (1) Index to County Birth Registers, Microfilm F14954, Provincial Archives of New Brunswick; (2) Acadia, Canada, Vital and Church Records (Drouin Collection), 1893-1898, Page 184.
Death: Deaths, Registration Division of Saint John City and County, New Brunswick.
Graveyard:

Jennie Gertrude Brown
Birth: Province of New Brunswick, Certificate of Registration of Death, Saint John City and County Sub-Health District.
Marriage:
Death: (1) Province of New Brunswick, Certificate of Registration of Death, Saint John City and County Sub-Health District; (2) Obituary, from the collection of James H. Williams and Helene Comeau Williams.
Graveyard: Listing of Interments prepared by Greenwood Cedar Hill Cemetery Company, Saint John West, Saint John, New Brunswick, November 2012.

Historical Accounts: (1) 1891 Census of Canada, Yarmouth, Nova Scotia, Page 21; (2) 1901 Census of Canada, Lancaster, Saint John, New Brunswick, Page 20; (3) 1911 Census of Canada, Lancaster, Saint John, New Brunswick, Page 20; (4) 1921 Census of Canada, Lancaster, Saint John, New Brunswick, Page 5; (5) 1940 Rural Preliminary List of Electors, Saint John-Albert, Rural Polling Division 146B, Page 2.

Charles Grierson Williams

(1876 - 1909)

Charles Grierson (commonly known by his middle name Grierson) was the fifth child of John Nelson Williams and Nancy Jane Coleman. He was born in Green Head, Saint John, New Brunswick, Canada in 1876. His exact date of birth is unknown at this time.

In the 1891 Census of Canada Charles Grierson was listed, at age sixteen, as living with his parents in Lancaster, Saint John, New Brunswick and working as a "cooper".

At age nineteen, on April 4, 1895, Charles Grierson was married to Agnes Jean Wade, also age nineteen, by Reverend J. W Corey at the home of his father, John Nelson Williams, in Randolph, Saint John, New Brunswick. His parents were listed as the official witnesses at the wedding ceremony. Charles Grierson was recorded as working as a "laborer" at the time of the marriage. Agnes Jean was born in Grand Bay, Saint John, New Brunswick on January 1, 1876 to Weston Wade and Margaret Smith.

Charles Grierson and Agnes Jean had five children together.

Elizabeth Dunham	b. April 22, 1895	d. December 27, 1956
Margaret	b. June 7, 1897	d. November 24, 1957
John Weston	b. May 6, 1900	d. November 11, 1943
Hazelle Revilo	b. January 16, 1906	d. December 15, 1977
Kenneth G.	*b. June 1908*	*d. August 23, 1913*

The 1901 Census of Canada recorded Agnes Jean, and her children Elizabeth Dunham, Margaret and John Weston as living with her parents in Lancaster. The location of Charles Grierson during that census is unknown.

At age thirty-four, on October 15, 1909, Charles Grierson, who was still working as a "laborer", died of "pleurisy" at his home in Milford, Saint John, New Brunswick. The location of his grave is unknown at this time.

When the 1911 Census of Canada was taken, Agnes Jean and her children were recorded as living in Lancaster at her mother's house. In that census Agnes Jean was listed as working as a "laundress".

On August 23, 1913 the fifth child of Charles Grierson and Agnes Jean, Kenneth G., died at the family home in Milford of "meningitis" at the age of five years and two months old. Where he was initially buried is not known. However, on September 30, 1917 his grandfather John Nelson Williams purchased a family plot, Lot 253, at the Old Cedar Hill Cemetery in Saint John

West, Saint John, New Brunswick and Kenneth G. was eventually reburied there in Grave 296.

Gravestone for Kenneth G. Williams
(Photograph from the collection of Jeffrey N. Williams and Jacqueline Pon Williams)

Agnes Jean and her children were recorded as living with her brother John Wade at 265 Duke Street in Lancaster at the time of the 1921 Census of Canada.

On February 28, 1923, Agnes Jean, age forty-seven, was married to her second husband, the widower Gifford Campbell Laurence age fifty-three in Fairville, Saint John, New Brunswick by W. M. Townsend, a Presbyterian minister. Gifford Campbell, the son of Robert Bruce Laurence and Agnes Grieg, was born in Leith, Scotland on August 23, 1869. There is no record of Agnes Jean and Gifford Campbell having any children together.

Gifford Campbell died on March 21, 1943 of "chronic myocarditis" in the Saint John General Hospital in Saint John City, Saint John, New Brunswick at the age of seventy-four. He was buried in Block 12, Plan 5 & 6, Lot 279 at the Greenwood Cemetery in Saint John West.

Agnes Jean lived to be seventy-one, dying of "coronary thrombosis" on May 7, 1947 in the Saint John General Hospital in Saint John City. At the time of her death, Agnes Jean was living at 178 Manawagonish Road in Fairville. Although her name is not listed onf the gravestone, the official cemetery records indicate that she was buried in the Greenwood Cemetery in Saint John West alongside her second husband in Block 12, Plan 5 & 6, Lot 279.

It should be noted the Cemetery records for Greenwood Cemetery indicate that Gifford Campbell Laurence's first name is misspelled on his gravestone.

Gravestone for Gifford Campbell Laurence
(Photograph from the collection of Jeffrey N. Williams and Jacqueline Pon Williams)

SOURCES:

Charles Grierson Williams
Birth:
Death: Deaths, Registration Division of Saint John City and County, New Brunswick.
Graveyard:

Agnes Jean Wade
Birth: Province of New Brunswick, Certificate of Registration of Death, Saint John City and County Sub-Health District.
Marriage: (1) Marriage, Registration Division of Saint John City and County, New Brunswick; (2) "Vital Statistics from Newspapers", by Daniel F. Johnson, Volume 100, Number 744, Provincial Archives of New Brunswick.
Death: Province of New Brunswick, Certificate of Registration of Death, Saint John City and County Sub-Health District.
Graveyard: (1) Listing of Interments prepared by Greenwood Cedar Hill Cemetery Company, Saint John West, Saint John, New Brunswick, September 2016; (2) Province of New Brunswick, Certificate of Registration of Death, Saint John City and County Sub-Health District.

Kenneth G. Williams
Birth:
Death: Deaths, Registration Division of Saint John City and County, New Brunswick.
Graveyard: Listing of Interments prepared by Greenwood Cedar Hill Cemetery Company, Saint John West, Saint John, New Brunswick, November 2012.

Gifford Campbell Laurence
Birth: Province of New Brunswick, Certificate of Registration of Death, Saint John City and County Sub-Health District.
Marriage: Province of New Brunswick, Department of Health, Official Notice of Marriage, Saint John City and County Sub-Health District.
Death: Province of New Brunswick, Certificate of Registration of Death, Saint John City and County Sub-Health District.
Graveyard: (1) Listing of Interments prepared by Greenwood Cedar Hill Cemetery Company, Saint John West, Saint John, New Brunswick, September 2016; (2) Province of New Brunswick, Certificate of Registration of Death, Saint John City and County Sub-Health District.

Historical Accounts: (1) 1891 Census of Canada, Lancaster, Saint John, New Brunswick, Page 113; ((2) 1901 Census of Canada, Lancaster, Saint John, New Brunswick, Page 32; (3) 1911 Census of Canada, Lancaster, Saint John, New Brunswick, Page 15; (4) 1921 Census of Canada, Lancaster, Saint John, New Brunswick, Page 11.

Emma Lillian Williams

(1878 - 1939)

The sixth child of John Nelson Williams and Nancy Jane Coleman was Emma Lillian (also known as Lilly). She was born on May 31, 1878 in Green Head, Saint John, New Brunswick, Canada.

On May 9, 1898, at age nineteen, Emma Lillian was married to the widower John Ervine Anderson, age twenty-two, in the Baptist Parsonage at Fairville, Saint John, New Brunswick by Reverend G. R. White. John Ervine, the son of Thomas Anderson and Agnes Smith, was born in Grand Bay, Saint John, New Brunswick on February 18, 1875. At the time of his marriage to Emma Lillian, John Ervine was working as a "lumberman".

Emma Lillian and John Ervine had two children together.

Ewen Wallace	*b. April 9, 1902*	*d. May 18, 1921*
Ruth Case	b. January 29, 1904	d. October 21, 1986

In the 1901 and 1911 Census' of Canada, Emma Lillian and John Ervine were recorded as living in Lancaster, Saint John, New Brunswick. John Ervine was listed as working as a "millman".

On May 18, 1921 the first of Emma Lillian and John Ervine's children, Ewen Wallace., died at the family home at 270 Guilford Street in Guy's Ward, Saint John, New Brunswick of "pulmonary tuberculosis' at the age of nineteen without having been married. At the time of his death Ewen Wallace was working as a "teamster in the trucking industry". He was buried on May 20, 1921 in Block 12, Plan 5 & 6, Lot 252 at the Greenwood Cemetery in Saint John West, Saint John, New Brunswick.

The 1921 Census of Canada, taken in June of that year, recorded Emma Lillian, John Ervine, their daughter Ruth Case and Emma Lillian's father, John Nelson Williams, living at 270 Guilford Street in Guy's Ward. John Ervine's occupation was listed as working in the "coal business".

John Ervine, at age fifty, died at his home at Hall's Lake in Musquash, Saint John, New Brunswick of "lobar pneumonia" on April 26, 1926. He was also buried at the Greenwood Cemetery in Saint John West in Block 12, Plan 5 & 6, Lot 252 on April 29, 1926.

On October 19, 1926, not quite six months after her first husband's death, Emma Lillian, then age forty-eight, was married to her second husband William George Thompson, age thirty-seven, in the Baptist Parsonage in Fairville by Reverend Clifford T. Clark. William George, born in Musquash on June 11, 1888, was the son of William Thompson and Mary Ann Totten. At the time of their marriage he was working as a "farmer". Emma Lillian and William George did not have any children together.

During his lifetime William George worked as a "road work laborer" in the Musquash area. He died at his home on Main Road in Musquash of "lobar pneumonia" on January 10, 1938 at the age of forty-nine. William George was buried on January 12, 1938 in St. Ann's Anglican Church Cemetery in Musquash, Saint John, New Brunswick.

Gravestone for William George Thompson
(Photograph from the collection of Jeffrey N. Williams and Jacqueline Pon Williams)

Emma Lillian outlived her second husband by a little more than one year, dying on April 27, 1939 at age sixty of "cardiac failure" in the Saint John General Hospital in Saint John City, Saint John, New Brunswick. Although her death record indicates she was buried in Musquash, the exact location of her burial has not been found.

SOURCES:

Emma Lillian Williams
Birth: Province of New Brunswick, Certificate of Registration of Death, Saint John City and County Sub-Health District.
Death: Province of New Brunswick, Certificate of Registration of Death, Saint John City and County Sub-Health District.
Graveyard:

John Ervine Anderson
Birth: Department of Health - New Brunswick, Certificate of Registration of Death, Saint John City and County Sub-Health District.
Marriage: (1) Marriage, Registration Division of Saint John City and County, New Brunswick; (2) Acadia, Canada, Vital and Church Records (Drouin Collection), 1891-1907, Schedule B – Marriages, Page 53.
Death: Department of Health - New Brunswick, Certificate of Registration of Death, Saint John City and County Sub-Health District.
Graveyard: Listing of Interments prepared by Greenwood Cedar Hill Cemetery Company, West Saint John, Saint John, New Brunswick, September 2016.

Ewen Wallace Anderson
Birth: Department of Health - New Brunswick, Certificate of Registration of Death, Saint John City and County Sub-Health District.
Death: Department of Health - New Brunswick, Certificate of Registration of Death, Saint John City and County Sub-Health District.
Graveyard: Listing of Interments prepared by Greenwood Cedar Hill Cemetery Company, West Saint John, Saint John, New Brunswick, September 2016.

William George Thompson
Birth: Province of New Brunswick, Certificate of Registration of Death, Saint John City and County Sub-Health District.
Marriage: Province of New Brunswick, Department of Health, Official Notice of Marriage, Saint John City and County Sub-Health District.
Death: Province of New Brunswick, Certificate of Registration of Death, Saint John City and County Sub-Health District.
Graveyard: Province of New Brunswick, Certificate of Registration of Death, Saint John City and County Sub-Health District.

Historical Accounts: (1) 1901 Census of Canada, Lancaster, Saint John, New Brunswick, Page 16; (2) 1911 Census of Canada, Lancaster, Saint John, New Brunswick, Page 12; (3) 1921 Census of Canada, Guy's Ward, Saint John, New Brunswick, Page 6.

Harry H. Williams

(1881 - 1902)

Harry H. was the seventh child of John Nelson Williams and Nancy Jane Coleman. He was born in Randolph, Saint John, New Brunswick, Canada on January 18, 1881.

In both the 1891 and 1901 Census' of Canada, Harry H. was recorded as living with his parents in Lancaster, Saint John, New Brunswick. In the 1901 census Harry H. was listed as working as a "teamster".

Harry H., age twenty-one, died on July 8, 1902 at home in Milford, Saint John, New Brunswick without issue. His cause of death was recorded as a "burst blood vessel". At the time of his death Harry H.'s occupation was listed as "millman". According to his Death Notice Harry H.'s funeral was held at his parents' home in Milford that same day at 2:30 P.M. The location of Harry H.'s burial is unknown.

SOURCES:

Harry H. Williams
Birth: 1901 Census of Canada, Lancaster, Saint John, New Brunswick, Page 21.
Death: (1) Deaths, Registration Division of Saint John City and County, New Brunswick; (2) Acadia, Canada, Vital and Church Records (Drouin Collection), 1901-1909, Page 16; (3) Death Notice, Saint John Globe, Tuesday, July 8, 1902, Page 8.
Graveyard:

Historical Accounts: (1) 1891 Census of Canada, Lancaster, Saint John, New Brunswick, Page 114; (2) 1901 Census of Canada, Lancaster, Saint John, New Brunswick, Page 21.

Ewen McFarlane Williams

(1883 - 1965)

Ewen McFarlane was the eighth child of John Nelson Williams and Nancy Jane Coleman. He was born in Green Head, Saint John, New Brunswick, Canada on August 26, 1883.

The 1901 Census of Canada recorded Ewen McFarlane, at age seventeen, living with his parents in Lancaster, Saint John, New Brunswick and working as a "millman".

On December 16, 1908, at age twenty-five, Ewen McFarlane was married to Perla C. Garrick, age twenty, at the Fairville Baptist Church in Fairville, Saint John, New Brunswick by Pastor Frank E. Bishop. Perla C., born on July 18, 1888, was the daughter of Andrew Garrick and Agnes Frederica Chipman of Saint John City, Saint John, New Brunswick. At the time of their marriage Ewen McFarlane was working as a "laborer".

Ewen McFarlane Williams and Perla C. Garrick
(Photograph from the collection of Jeffrey N. Williams and Jacqueline Pon Williams)

Ewen McFarlane and Perla C. had eight children together.

Wenonah Bernice	b. February 13, 1910	d. October 10, 2008
Lillian Helena	b. July 24, 1911	d. March 12, 2010
Harry Nelson	b. December 2, 1912	d. December 15, 1985
Gordon Ronald	b. June 12, 1914	d. January 25, 1979
Muriel C.	b. April 12, 1916	d. February 11, 2013

Ewen Mansfield	b. November 4, 1918	d.
Malcolm Vernon	b. March 18, 1922	d. July 11, 1941
Shirley Dorothy	b. September 25, 1924	d. June 6, 1996

In the 1911 Census of Canada, Ewen McFarlane, Perla C. and their first child, Wenonah Bernice, were recorded as living in Milford, Saint John, New Brunswick. Ewen McFarlane was working as a "teamster" at a lumber mill when that census was taken.

At the time of the 1921 Census of Canada, Ewen McFarlane, Perla C. and their first six children had moved and were living in Kingsville, Saint John, New Brunswick. Ewen McFarlane's occupation was listed as working in a saw mill as a "laborer".

In early 1923, seeking work, Ewen McFarlane traveled to Madison, Somerset, Maine, USA, where his sisters Bessie D. (Williams) Golding and Mary B. (Williams) Gilbert and their families were living. Later that year on September 25, 1923, after Ewen McFarlane established himself and gained employment as a "painter", Perla C. and their seven children moved to Madison to join him. They traveled via the Canadian Pacific railroad and entered the United States through Vanceboro, Washington, Maine.

When the 1930 United States Federal Census of Madison was taken, Ewen McFarlane and Perla C. were recorded as living at 9 Gray Street, next door to his sister Bessie D. and her husband Malcolm C. Golding. Their house was also down the street from his aunt Idell Cordelia Williams and her husband Thomas Perly Otis and around the block from his sister Mary B. and her husband Leroy Franklin Gilbert. In that census Ewen McFarlane was working as a "laborer" in a pulp mill.

The 1940 United States Federal Census recorded Ewen McFarlane, Perla C. and four of their children as still living at 9 Gray Street in Madison. Ewen McFarlane's occupation was listed as a "painter" in a woolen mill.

In their later years, around 1953, Ewen McFarlane and Perla C. moved to Hayward, Alameda, California to be in a warmer climate and near their daughter Shirley Dorothy (Williams) Jordan and her family.

Ewen McFarlane died at age eighty-one on January 18, 1965 at Fairmont Hospital in San Leandro, Alameda, California. His cause of death was listed as "chronic pulmonary emphysema". At the time of his death Ewen McFarlane and Perla C. were living at 179 Poplar Street in Hayward. His funeral service was held on Wednesday, January 20, 1965. Ewen McFarlane's body was sent back to Maine where he was buried in Lot 631 at the Forest Hill Cemetery in Madison.

Perla C. outlived her husband by more than seven years, dying on December 19, 1972 at age eighty-four at her home on Popular Street in Hayward. The cause of her death was recorded as “cardiac failure”. Her funeral was held at 2:00 P.M. on Friday, December 22, 1972 at the Guerrero & Seramur Mortuary in San Leandro. Perla C.’s body was also sent back to Maine for burial in Lot 631at the Forest Hill Cemetery in Madison.

Williams Family Plot Marker, Forest Hill Cemetery, Madison, Maine (top) and Headstones for Ewen McFarlane Williams (bottom left) and Perla C. Garrick (bottom right)
(Photographs from the collection of Jeffrey N. Williams and Jacqueline Pon Williams)

SOURCES:

Ewen McFarlane Williams
Birth: (1) U.S., Social Security Death Index, 1935-2014 (database on-line), Provo, Utah, USA: Ancestry.com Operations Inc., 2011; (2) California Death Index 1940 to 1997 (database on-line), Provo, Utah, USA: Ancestry.com Operations Inc., 2000.
Death: (1) Certificate of Death, State of California, Department of Public Health; (2) U.S., Social Security Death Index, 1935-2014 (database on-line), Provo, Utah, USA: Ancestry.com Operations Inc., 2011; (3) California Death Index 1940 to 1997 (database on-line), Provo, Utah, USA: Ancestry.com Operations Inc., 2000; (4) Obituary, The Daily Review, Hayward, California, Tuesday, January 19, 1965; Page 6.
Graveyard: (1) Records for Forest Hill Cemetery managed by the Town of Madison Maine; (2) “Forest Hill Cemetery”, updated by Dassie Jackson and Lena Arno in 2002 and 2003, page 162, Madison Historical Society.

Perla C. Garrick
Birth: (1) U.S., Social Security Applications and Claim Index, 1936-2007 (database on-line), Provo, Utah, USA: Ancestry.com Operations Inc., 2015; (2) California Death Index 1940 to 1997 (database on-line), Provo, Utah, USA: Ancestry.com Operations Inc., 2000; (3) 1901 Census of Canada, Sydney Ward, Saint John, New Brunswick, Page 26.
Marriage: (1) Official Notice of Marriage, Province of New Brunswick; (2) Acadia, Canada, Vital and Church Records (Drouin Collection), 1908-1919, Schedule B – Marriages, Page 15.
Death: (1) Certificate of Death, State of California, Department of Public Health; (2) California Death Index 1940 to 1997 (database on-line), Provo, Utah, USA: Ancestry.com Operations Inc., 2000; (3) Obituary, Oakland Tribune, Oakland, California, Friday, December 22, 1972; Page 18.
Graveyard: (1) Records for Forest Hill Cemetery managed by the Town of Madison Maine; (2) "Forest Hill Cemetery", updated by Dassie Jackson and Lena Arno in 2002 and 2003, page 162, Madison Historical Society.

Historical Accounts: (1) 1911 Census of Canada, Lancaster, Saint John, New Brunswick, Page 12; (2) 1921 Census of Canada, Lancaster, Saint John, New Brunswick, Page 20; (3) 1930 United States Federal Census for Madison, Somerset, Maine, Page 10A; (4) 1940 United States Federal Census for Madison, Somerset, Maine, Page 16A; (5) Letter from Ewen Mansfield Williams to James Harold Williams and Helene Comeau Williams, January 24, 2004, from the collection of James Harold Williams and Helene Comeau Williams.

Jennie Graves Williams

(1886 - 1936)

The ninth child of John Nelson Williams and Nancy Jane Coleman was Jennie Graves. She was born on October 21, 1886 in Pokiok, Saint John, New Brunswick, Canada.

At age nineteen, on July 31, 1906, Jennie Graves was married to William Thomas Stout age twenty-five by David Long, Clergyman, in the United Baptist Parsonage on Victoria Street, Saint John City, Saint John, New Brunswick. William Thomas, who was working as a "bandsaw filer" at the time of their wedding, was born on April 4, 1881 in Milford, Saint John, New Brunswick to William Stout and Anderina Wilson.

Jennie Graves and William Thomas had eight children together.

Horace Nelson	b. April 4, 1907	d. February 10, 1964
Ruby Jean	b. June 17, 1908	d. February 2, 1980
William Alexander	b. December 1909	d. November 4, 1972
James Murray	b. November 14, 1911	d. December 19, 1973
George Robert	b. February 14, 1914	d. May 5, 1991
Gertrude Andrena	b. April 12, 1918	d. May 2, 1989
John Edward	b. May 20, 1920	d. September 25, 1954
Florence Mary	b. 1923	d.

The 1911 and 1921 Census' of Canada recorded Jennie Graves, William Thomas and their family as living in Lancaster, Saint John, New Brunswick. In those census' Williams Thomas was listed as working as a "saw filer" in a lumber mill.

On October 27, 1936, Jennie Graves died at Saint Joseph Hospital in Saint John City at the age of fifty. Her cause of death was listed as "coronary thrombosis". She was buried at the Cedar Hill Cemetery Extension, Section C, Lot 60 A E1/2 in Saint John West, Saint John, New Brunswick.

The 1940 Rural List of Electors for the Parish of Lancaster Rural Polling Division No. 146B recorded William Thomas, a "millman" as being from Milford.

At the age of fifty-nine William Thomas was married to his second wife, the widow Agnes (McIntyre) Totten, age fifty-two, on November 21, 1941 in Fairville, Saint John, New Brunswick by Reverend Frank H. Sinnott. Agnes, the daughter of William McIntyre and Isabelle Stewart, was born in Scotland in 1889. The exact date and place of her birth have not been found.

When the 1949 Rural List of Electors for Milford and the 1957 and 1963 Urban Preliminary Lists of Electors for Lancaster were published, William Thomas and his second wife Agnes were recorded as living at 310 Milford Road in Milford.

William Thomas died on June 15, 1970 at the age of eighty-nine. The place and cause of his death have not been found. He was also buried in Section C, Lot 60 A E1/2 at the Cedar Hill Cemetery Extension in Saint John West.

Additional information regarding the life and death of Agnes has not been found.

Gravestone for Jennie Graves Williams and William Thomas Stout
(Photograph from the collection of Jeffrey N. Williams and Jacqueline Pon Williams)

SOURCES:

Jennie Graves Williams
Birth: (1) Province of New Brunswick, Certificate of Registration of Death, Saint John City and County Sub-Health District; (2) 1901 Census of Canada, Parish of Lancaster, Saint John, New Brunswick, Page 21.
Death: Province of New Brunswick, Certificate of Registration of Death, Saint John City and County Sub-Health District.
Graveyard: Listing of Interments prepared by Greenwood Cedar Hill Cemetery Company, Saint John West, Saint John, New Brunswick, November 2012.

William Thomas Stout
Birth: Late Registration of Birth, Province of New Brunswick, Canada.
Marriage: (1) Marriage, Registration Division of Saint John City and County, New Brunswick; (2) Acadia, Canada, Vital and Church Records (Drouin Collection), 1891-1907, Page 161.
Death: Listing of Interments prepared by Greenwood Cedar Hill Cemetery Company, Saint John West, Saint John, New Brunswick, November 2012.
Graveyard: Listing of Interments prepared by Greenwood Cedar Hill Cemetery Company, Saint John West, Saint John, New Brunswick, November 2012.

Agnes McIntyre
Birth:
Marriage: Province of New Brunswick, Department of Health, Official Notice of Marriage, Saint John City and County Sub-Health District.
Death:

Historical Accounts: (1) 1901 Census of Canada, Parish of Lancaster, Saint John, New Brunswick, Page 21; (2) 1911 Census of Canada, Parish of Lancaster, Saint John, New Brunswick, Page 10; (3) 1921 Census of Canada, Parish of Lancaster, Saint John, New Brunswick, Page 11; (4) 1940 Rural Preliminary List of Electors, Saint John-Albert, Rural Polling Division 146B, Parish of Lancaster, Page 2; (5) 1949 Rural Preliminary List of Electors, Electoral District of Saint John-Albert, Rural Polling Division 177, Milford, Page 2; (6) 1957 Urban Preliminary List of Electors, Electoral District of Saint John-Albert, City of Lancaster, Urban Polling Division No. 184B, Page 1; (7) 1963 Urban Preliminary List of Electors, Electoral District of Saint John-Albert, City of Lancaster, Urban Polling Division No. 196, Page 2.

Mary B. Williams

(1890 - 1963)

Mary B., the tenth child of John Nelson Williams and Nancy Jane Coleman, was born in Saint John County, New Brunswick, Canada on June 4, 1890.

On November 12, 1910, Mary B. crossed the United States border at Vanceboro, Washington, Maine on her way to Madison, Somerset, Maine. In the "Manifest for Admission" she was described as being 5' 8" tall with a light complexion, brown hair and hazel eyes. Her occupation at that time was listed as a "domestic".

At the age of twenty-one, Mary B. was to married Leroy Franklin Gilbert, age twenty, in Madison on March 23, 1912 by George B. Southwick, a Clergyman. Leroy Franklin was born to Charles Franklin Gilbert and Carrie Dunphy of Madison on October 21, 1891. At the time of their marriage Leroy Franklin was working as a "paper mill operator".

Mary B. and Leroy Franklin had five children together.

Charles Franklin	b. March 29, 1913	d. October 23, 1980
John Nelson	b. July 25, 1914	d. August 23, 1997
Gordon Leslie	b. December 13, 1916	d. September 15, 1971
Archie McKenzie	*b. January 9, 1920*	*d. June 6, 1936*
Jean F.	b. June 22, 1929	d.

On June 5, 1917 Leroy Franklin completed his "Registration Card" for the United States World War I draft. In that document he was described as having medium height, being of medium build, with blue eyes and brown hair. His occupation was listed as a "teamster" working for the Great Northern Paper Company in Madison.

In the 1920 United States Federal Census of Madison, Mary B. and Leroy Franklin were recorded as living next door to her sister Bessie D. Williams and her husband Malcolm C. Golding on Gray Street in Madison. Leroy Franklin's occupation was listed as working in a "paper mill" in that census.

The 1930 United States Federal Census of Madison recorded that Mary B. and Leroy Franklin had moved and were then living on Houghton Street in Madison. This house was around the block from Mary B.'s sister Bessie D. Williams and her husband Malcolm Campbell Golding, her brother Ewen Mansfield Williams and his wife Perla C. Garrick, and down the street from her aunt Idell Cordelia Williams and her husband Thomas Perly Otis.

On Friday evening June 24, 1932 Leroy Franklin, while taking his turn at bat in a baseball game between the Madison Fire Department and the Madison Ramblers, was accidentally struck behind his right ear with a ball pitched by Arthur Willette. Although he remained on the sidelines for the rest of the game, and drove himself home when it was over, he died at his home later that evening from what was later determined to be a "double fracture of the skull". Leroy Franklin was just forty years old.

At the time of his death Leroy Franklin was the Chief of Police for the City of Madison, a position he had held for almost ten years. Besides being the police chief he was also a Second Lieutenant with the Madison Fire Department and had previously been a Deputy Sheriff for Somerset County.

The funeral for Leroy Franklin was held at 2:00 P.M. on Tuesday, June 27, 1932 at the Congregational Church in Madison with Reverend E. C. Evans officiating. The funeral announcement in the Lewiston Evening Journal indicated that "…over 400 friends and relatives assembled to pay their last tribute to Mr. Gilbert…" Leroy Franklin was subsequently buried in Lot 690 at the Forest Hill Cemetery in Madison. At his graveside the Indian Springs Lodge I.O.O.F., of which Leroy Franklin who was a member, conducted a service and Chief Daniel M. Nichols, Arthur Heald, Martelle Perkins and Clifford Daggett from the Madison Fire Department acted as pallbearers.

Almost four years later, the fourth child of Mary B. and Leroy Franklin, Archie McKenzie died on June 6, 1936, at the age of sixteen, in Madison of an "accidental drowning". He was also buried in Lot 690 at Forest Hill Cemetery in Madison.

When the 1940 United States Federal Census was taken Mary B. and her children were still living at the family home at 17 Houghton Street in Madison.

Shortly after the 1940 census was taken Mary B. started working at Good Will – Hinckley Homes for Boys and Girls just outside of Fairfield, Somerset, Maine. On April 21, 1941 she wrote to her nephew Harold Edger Williams in Saint John County, New Brunswick, Canada letting him know that she had been working at Good Will – Hinckley for "almost a year" and among other family news that her daughter Jean F. was living with her.

Mary B. survived Leroy Franklin by thirty-three years dying at the age of seventy-three in Portland, Cumberland, Maine on October 27, 1963 from "cardiac arrhythmia". She too was buried in Lot 690 at the Forest Hill Cemetery in Madison.

SOURCES:

Mary B. Williams
Birth: U.S., Social Security Applications and Claims Index, 1936-2007 [database on-line]. Provo, UT, USA: Ancestry.com Operations, Inc., 2015.
Death: (1) Maine State Archives Death Database; (2) Maine Death Index, 1960-1997 [database on-line]. Provo, UT, USA: Ancestry.com Operations, Inc., 2002.
Graveyard: (1) Records for Forest Hill Cemetery managed by the Town of Madison, Maine; (2) "Forest Hill Cemetery", updated by Dassie Jackson and Lena Arno in 2002 and 2003, page 55, Madison Historical Society.

Leroy Franklin Gilbert
Birth: U.S., World War I Draft Registration Cards, 1917-1918 [database on-line]. Provo, UT, USA: Ancestry.com Operations, Inc., 2005.
Marriage: Record of a Marriage, Maine Vital Records.
Death: (1) Death Announcement, The Lewiston Daily Sun, Lewiston, Maine, Saturday, June 25, 1932, Page 1; (2) Funeral Announcement, Lewiston Evening Journal, Tuesday, June 28, 1932, Page 2; (3) "History of Madison Maine" Compiled from Historical Notes by Emma Folsom Clark, Page 315, Picton Press 2003.
Graveyard: (1) Records for Forest Hill Cemetery managed by the Town of Madison, Maine; (2) "Forest Hill Cemetery", updated by Dassie Jackson and Lena Arno in 2002 and 2003, page 55, Madison Historical Society.

Archie McKenzie Gilbert
Birth: Record of a Birth, Maine Vital Records.
Death: (1) Madison Maine Death Records, Page 145, Town of Madison, Maine; (2) "History of Madison Maine" Compiled from Historical Notes by Emma Folsom Clark, Page 325, Picton Press 2003.
Graveyard: (1) Records for Forest Hill Cemetery managed by the Town of Madison, Maine; (2) "Forest Hill Cemetery", updated by Dassie Jackson and Lena Arno in 2002 and 2003, page 55, Madison Historical Society.

Historical Accounts: (1) 1920 United States Federal Census for Madison, Somerset, Maine, Page 2B; (2) 1930 United States Federal Census for Madison, Somerset, Maine, Page 10A; (3) 1940 United States Federal Census for Anson, Somerset, Maine, Page 15B; (4) List or Manifest of Alien Passengers Applying for Admission, Border Crossings from Canada to U.S., 1895-1956: (5) U.S., Border Crossings from Canada to U.S., 1825-1960 [database on-line]. Provo, UT, USA: Ancestry.com Operations, Inc., 2010; (6) Letter from Mary B. Williams Gilbert to Harold Edger Williams, April 21, 1941, from the collection of James Harold Williams and Helene Comeau Williams.

Percy B. Williams

(1879 – 1962)

The first child of Silas M. Williams and his first wife Mary Ann Brown was Percy B. He was born on December 22, 1879 in Nelson, Northumberland, New Brunswick, Canada.

When the 1901 Census of Canada was taken, Percy B., then age twenty-one, was recorded as living with his parents in Nelson and working as a "millman".

By the time the 1910 United States Federal Census was taken Percy B. had moved from Canada to the city of Oconto in Oconto County, Wisconsin, USA where he was recorded as living with Margaret J. Flett, the sister of his step-mother, and her husband Robert MacGregor Fleming and was listed as their "nephew". In that census Percy B.'s occupation was listed as a "plumber at a plumbing shop".

On June 21, 1916 Percy B., age thirty-six, married Clara J. Fleming, age twenty-five, in Oconto. Clara J. the daughter of his step-aunt and uncle, the aforementioned Margaret J. Flett and her husband Robert MacGregor Fleming, was born on August 28, 1890 in Manistee, Manistee County, Michigan.

Percy B. and Clara J. had two children together.

Margaret Jane	*b. 1917*	*d. March 9, 1918*
Mary Jean	b. May 23, 1920	d. September 26, 2010

The first child born to Percy B. and Clara J. died of an unknown cause when she was around one year old. She was buried on March 12, 1918 in Block 41, Lot 16 at the Evergreen Cemetery in Oconto.

On September 12, 1918 Percy B. registered for the United States World War I Draft. In that document he listed his occupation as "steam fitter and plumber" with Percy Williams & Co. in Oconto.

In 1920 United States Federal Census, which was taken in January of that year, Percy B., still working as a "plumber", Clara J. and his father-in-law Robert Fleming were recorded as living at 522 Main Street in Oconto.

On Friday November 3, 1920 the Oconto Falls Herald published a notification that Percy B. had applied to become a naturalized citizen of the United States of America. His application was subsequently approved and he became a naturalized citizen of the United States on November 13, 1920. In that document his residential address was recorded as 522 Main Street, Oconto.

In the Thursday March 1, 1923 edition of the Oconto County Reporter it was published that "Percy Williams has moved his plumbing establishment from 216 Park Avenue to the building on Main Street formerly occupied by Christ Meurer, tailor."

When the 1930 and 1940 United States Federal Census' were taken Percy B., Clara J. and their daughter, Mary Jean, were recorded as still living in Oconto. Percy B.'s occupation was again recorded as a "plumber at a plumbing shop".

Percy B. registered for the World War II draft on April 25, 1942. In that document he was described as being 5' 5" tall, 130 pounds, with brown eyes, gray hair and a light complexion. He also reported his residential address as 522 Main Street, Oconto and that he was "self-employed".

On September 6, 1962, at the age of eighty-two, Percy B. died at the Oconto Hospital in Oconto. The cause of his death was listed as "heart attack". His funeral was held at 2:30 P.M. on Sunday September 9 at the Oconto Presbyterian Church in Oconto with Reverend Newton Roberts officiating. Percy B. was buried in Block 41, Lot 16 at the Evergreen Cemetery in Oconto on September 9, 1962.

During his life Percy B. was a member of the Masons, Royal Arch Masons and Knights Templar. The Knights Templar formed an honor guard for him at both his funeral and his burial.

On Wednesday, June 27, 1973 The Oconto County Reporter announced that Clara J. had been admitted to the Oconto Memorial Hospital the previous Saturday, June 23. No additional information was given.

Clara J. outlived her husband by more than fourteen years dying on December 11, 1976, at the age of eighty-six, at the Riverside Nursing Home in Oconto after a "short illness". Her funeral service, with Reverend John Lyford officiating, was held at the First Presbyterian Church in Oconto on Monday December 13, 1976. She too was buried in Block 41, Lot 16 at the Evergreen Cemetery in Oconto.

SOURCES:

Percy B. Williams
Birth: (1) Births, Registration Division of Northumberland County, New Brunswick; (2) "Canada, Births and Baptisms, 1661-1959," index, FamilySearch, (https://familysearch.org/pal:/MM9.1.1/F2D4-KBK).
Death: (1) Wisconsin Death Index, 1959-1997, Page K 11; (2) "U.S., Social Security Death Index, 1935-Current (database on-line), Provo, UT; Ancestry.com Operations Inc, 2011.; (3) Obituary, Oconto County Reporter, September 13, 1962, Page 2; (4) Obituary, Green Bay Press Gazette, Green Bay, Wisconsin, September 8, 1962, Page 16.
Graveyard: Evergreen Cemetery Book, Oconto County WIGenWeb Project.

Clara J. Fleming
Birth: (1) "U.S., Social Security Death Index, 1935-Current (database on-line), Provo, UT; Ancestry.com Operations Inc, 2011; (2) Obituary, Green Bay Press Gazette, Green Bay, Wisconsin, Sunday December 12, 1976, Page 73.
Marriage: Obituary, Green Bay Press Gazette, Green Bay, Wisconsin, Sunday December 12, 1976, Page 73.
Death: (1) Wisconsin Death Index, 1959-1997, Page B 11; (2) "U.S., Social Security Death Index, 1935-Current (database on-line), Provo, UT; Ancestry.com Operations Inc, 2011; (3) Obituary, Green Bay Press Gazette, Green Bay, Wisconsin, Sunday December 12, 1976, Page 73.
Graveyard: Evergreen Cemetery Book, Oconto County WIGenWeb Project.

Margaret Jane Williams
Birth:
Death: Evergreen Cemetery Book, Oconto County WIGenWeb Project.
Graveyard: Evergreen Cemetery Book, Oconto County WIGenWeb Project.

Historical Accounts: (1) 1881 Census of Canada, Nelson, Northumberland, New Brunswick, Page 52; (2) 1891 Census of Canada, Nelson, Northumberland, New Brunswick; (3) 1900 United States Federal Census for Manistee, Manistee, Michigan, Page 10; (4) 1901 Census of Canada, Nelson, Northumberland, New Brunswick, Page 7; (5) 1910 United States Federal Census for Oconto, Oconto, Wisconsin, Page 4A; (6) 1920 United States Federal Census for Oconto, Oconto, Wisconsin, Page 2B; (7) 1930 United States Federal Census for Oconto, Oconto, Wisconsin, Page 1B; (8) 1940 United States Federal Census for Oconto, Oconto, Wisconsin, Page 5B; (9) Illinois, Northern District, Naturalization Index, 1840-1950, Image 1944; (10) United States World War I Draft Registration Cards, 1917-1918; (11) United States World War II Draft Registration Cards, 1942; (12) Obituary, Oconto County Reporter, September 13, 1962, Page 2; (13) Death Notice, Green Bay Press Gazette, Green Bay, Wisconsin, Saturday, September 8, 1962, Page 2; (14) Newspaper article, Oconto Falls Herald, Oconto Falls, Wisconsin, Friday, November 3, 1920, Page 2; (15) Newspaper article, Oconto County Reporter, Thursday, March 1, 1923, Page 1; (16) Newspaper article, Oconto County Reporter, Wednesday, June 27, 1973, Section I, Page 3.

Bessie Williams

(1882 – 1939)

Bessie, the second child of Silas M. Williams and his first wife Mary Ann Brown, was born on January 20, 1882 in Nelson, Northumberland, New Brunswick, Canada.

In the 1911 Census of Canada Bessie, then age twenty-nine, was recorded as living with her parents in Nelson and working in "tailoring".

At the age of thirty-one Bessie was married to Earl Stanley Saunders, age twenty-two, on July 12, 1913 by Reverend W. J. Bate, the Rector of the Church of St. Andrew's in Northumberland County, New Brunswick. Earl Stanley, born on July 15, 1890 in Kirkwood, Northumberland, New Brunswick, was the son of Allan Alexander Mason Saunders and Eliza Henderson. At the time of their marriage Earl Stanley was "farming" in Kirkwood.

During their marriage Bessie and Earl Stanley had seven children together.

Kathleen Helen	b. March 16, 1914	d. March 18, 2002
Reginald Allan	b. June 1, 1915	d. December 16, 1979
Jean Alexis	b. May 1, 1917	d. October 17, 1995
Keith	*b. March 29, 1920*	*d. November 9, 1933*
Lambert William	b. 1922	d. November 24, 1984
Harold R.	b. June 20, 1924	d. July 9, 2003
Allan Wilson	b. February 15, 1926	d. November 6, 1993

Bessie Williams (left) and Earl Stanley Saunders (right)
(Photograph Courtesy of Earl Stanley Saunders)

When the 1921 Census of Canada was taken Bessie, Earl Stanley and their first four children were recorded as living in Nelson with Earl Stanley working as a "laborer".

The fourth child of Bessie and Earl Stanley, Keith, died of "acute appendicitis" when he was thirteen years three months old on November 9, 1933 at the Miramichi Hospital in Miramichi, Northumberland, New Brunswick. His funeral was held the following day, November 10, 1933, at 3:00 P.M. at his parents' home with Reverend H.M. Alexander presiding. Keith was buried in the Saunders Cemetery, Chelmsford, Northumberland, New Brunswick in Row 3, Plot 33 of the Old Section. It should be noted here that the birth certificate for Keith listed his name as "Blair Earle Mason Saunders". However, his death certificate, death notice, obituary, gravestone and the 1921 Census of Canada all recorded his name as Keith Saunders.

In the 1935 Canadian Voter List for the Electoral District of Northumberland, Bessie and Earl Stanley were recorded as living and farming in Chelmsford.

On May 18, 1939, Bessie died at the age of fifty-seven at the Miramichi Hospital in Miramichi after receiving treatment there for ten days. Her cause of death was recorded as "lobar pneumonia". Her funeral was held at her home on Saturday afternoon May 20, 1939. She was buried that same day in in Row 3, Plot 33 of the Old Section at the Saunders Cemetery.

The 1940, 1945, 1949 and 1953 Canadian Voter Lists for the Electoral District of Northumberland recorded Earl Stanley living and working as a "laborer" in his hometown of Kirkwood.

Earl Stanley, outliving his wife by more than eighteen years, died at the age of sixty-seven on December 14, 1957 at the Valley Home in Kirkwood after a lengthy illness. His specific cause of death was recorded as "leukemia". Funeral services for Earl Stanley were held on Monday December 16, 1957 at 2:00 P.M. with Reverend J. E. Morgan presiding. He was buried in row 3 of the Old Section at the Saunders Cemetery.

SOURCES:

Bessie Williams
Birth: (1) Births, Registration Division of Northumberland County, New Brunswick; (2) New Brunswick, Provincial Returns of Births and Late Registrations, 1810-1906," database with images FamilySearch (https://familysearch.org/ark:/61903/1:1:XTQM-Q6P:2 January 2015); (3) Acadia, Canada, Vital and Church Records (Drouin Collection), 1888-1919, Page 52.
Death: (1) Province of New Brunswick, Certificate of Registration of Death, Northumberland Sub-Health District; (2) Obituary, North Shore News, Friday, May 19, 1939.
Graveyard: "Cemeteries of the Parish of Nelson, Northumberland County, Province of New Brunswick, Canada", Page 36, NB Genealogical Society-Miramichi Branch, 2002.

Earl Stanley Saunders
Birth: Province of New Brunswick, Certificate of Registration of Death, Northumberland Sub-Health District.
Marriage: (1) Marriage, Registration Division County of Northumberland, New Brunswick; (2) Acadia, Canada, Vital and Church Records (Drouin Collection), 1888-1919, Page 131.
Death: (1) Province of New Brunswick, Certificate of Registration of Death, Northumberland Sub-Health District; (2) Obituary, North Shore Ledger.
Graveyard: "Cemeteries of the Parish of Nelson, Northumberland County, Province of New Brunswick, Canada", Page 36, NB Genealogical Society-Miramichi Branch, 2002.

Keith Saunders
Birth: Province of New Brunswick, Department of Health, Certificate of Registration of Birth, Northumberland Sub-Health District
Death: (1) Department of Health – New Brunswick, Certificate of Registration of Death, Northumberland Sub-Health District; (2) Obituary, Miramichi Branch, The New Brunswick Genealogical Society, Obituary Database; (3) Death Notice, North Shore Leader, Friday, November 17, 1933.
Graveyard: "Cemeteries of the Parish of Nelson, Northumberland County, Province of New Brunswick, Canada", Page 36, NB Genealogical Society-Miramichi Branch, 2002.

Historical Accounts: (1) 1911 Census of Canada, Nelson, Northumberland, New Brunswick, Page 15; (2) 1921 Census of Canada, Nelson, Northumberland, New Brunswick, Page 23; (3) Canada, Voter Lists, 1935 List of Electors, Electoral District of Northumberland, N.B., Rural Polling Division No. 41, Parish of Nelson, Page 2; (4) Canada, Voter Lists, 1940 Rural Preliminary List of Electors, Electoral District of Northumberland, Rural Polling Division No. 41, Chelmsford, Page 2; (5) Canada, Voter Lists, 1945 Rural Preliminary List of Electors, Electoral District of Northumberland, Rural Polling Division No. 41, Chelmsford, Page 2; (6) Canada, Voter Lists, 1949 Rural Preliminary List of Electors, Electoral District of Northumberland, Rural Polling Division No. 41, Chelmsford, Page 2; (7) Canada, Voter Lists, 1953 Rural Preliminary List of Electors, Electoral District of Northumberland, Rural Polling Division No. 43, McKinleyville, Page 2.

Helen Gertrude Williams

(1885 – 1977)

The third child, Helen Gertrude, of Silas M. Williams and his first wife Mary Ann Brown was born on July 2, 1885 in Nelson, Northumberland, New Brunswick, Canada.

When the 1901 Census of Canada was taken Helen Gertrude, then age fifteen, was recorded as living with her father and his second wife Elizabeth Flett in Nelson.

In the "U.S. Records of Aliens Pre-Examines in Canada" for August 8, 1918 Helen Gertrude declared that she had been living in Boston, Suffolk, Massachusetts, USA from 1902, when she was sixteen, through July 10, 1918. She was described in that document as being 5' 4" tall, weighing 125 pounds, with brown hair, brown eyes and a dark complexion.

The 1920 United States Federal Census recorded Helen Gertrude living at 616 Dudley Street in Boston.

On April 9, 1929, Helen Gertrude filed her "Declaration of Intention" to become a citizen of the United States of America with the District Court of the United States in Boston. In that document she indicated that she was working as a "waitress" and resided at 519 Audubon Road in Boston. She was still living at that address when the 1930 United States Federal Census was taken. Helen Gertrude's petition for citizenship was granted on June 4, 1934.

Sometime between 1934 and 1977 Helen Gertrude returned to Canada, where, on Wednesday, August 31, 1977, she died at the age of ninety-two at the Saint John West Community Hospital in Saint John West, Saint John, New Brunswick after "a period of failing health". No record has been found to indicate that she ever married or had children. A funeral was held for Helen Gertrude at the Castle Funeral Home in Saint John West Saturday September 3rd at 2:00 PM. On September 6, 1977 her cremains were buried at Fernhill Cemetery in East Saint John, Saint John, New Brunswick in Block VIII, Delphinium Path, Lot 6167-A, Grave 1-C.

SOURCES:

Helen Gertrude Williams
Birth: (1) Births, Registration Division of Northumberland County, New Brunswick; (2) New Brunswick, Provincial Returns of Births and Late Registrations, 1810-1906," database with images FamilySearch (https://familysearch.org/ark:/61903/1:1:XTQM-829: 12 December 2014); (3) Acadia, Canada, Vital and Church Records (Drouin Collection), 1888-1919, Page 52.
Death: (1) Death Notice, Saint John Evening Times Globe, Thursday, September 1, 1977, Page 27; (2) U.S., Social Security Death Index, 1935-Current [database on-line], Provo, UT, USA: Ancestry.com Operations, Inc., 2011; (3) Interment Record provided by Fernhill Cemetery Company, East Saint John, Saint John, New Brunswick.
Graveyard: Interment Record provided by Fernhill Cemetery Company, East Saint John, Saint John, New Brunswick.

Historical Accounts: (1) 1901 Census of Canada, Nelson, Northumberland, New Brunswick, Page 7; (2) United States Records of Aliens Pre-Examined in Canada, 1917-1954, August 8, 1918; (3) 1920 United States Federal Census for Boston, Suffolk, Massachusetts, Page 4A; (4) 1930 United States Federal Census for Boston, Suffolk, Massachusetts, Page 13B; (5) U.S. Department of Labor Naturalization Service Declaration of Intension, Document Number 219355; (6) United States of America, Petition for Citizenship, Document Number 152908.

John James Williams

(1893 – 1915)

John James was the first child of Silas M. Williams and his second wife Elizabeth Flett. He was born on October 26, 1893 in Nelson, Northumberland New Brunswick, Canada.

In the 1911 Census of Canada John James, then age seventeen, was recorded as working in a drug store and living with his parents in Nelson.

On April 23, 1915 at the age of twenty-one, John James died at home in Nelson of "consumption" having never married or had children. At the time of his death he was working as a "drug clerk" at A. E. Shaw's Pharmacy. On Sunday April 25, 1915 John James' funeral services were held at both the family home and the grave with Reverend Alex Firth presiding. In his obituary it said John James "…was highly respected by all who knew him…" and that his funeral was "…very largely attended". John James was buried in his father's family plot at the St. James United Cemetery in Nelson.

SOURCES:

John James Williams
Birth: (1) Births, Registration Division of Northumberland County, New Brunswick; (2) Acadia, Canada, Vital and Church Records (Drouin Collection), 1888-1918, Page 45; (3) Index to County Birth Registers, Microfilm F14023, Provincial Archives of New Brunswick.
Death: (1) Deaths, Registration Division of Northumberland County, New Brunswick; (2) Obituary, North Shore Ledger.
Graveyard: "Cemeteries of the Parish of Nelson, Northumberland County, Province of New Brunswick, Canada", Page 55, NB Genealogical Society-Miramichi Branch, 2002.

Historical Accounts: (1) 1911 Census of Canada, Nelson, Northumberland, New Brunswick, Page 15; (2) Obituary, North Shore Ledger.

Silas Leslie Williams

(1898 – 1970)

The second child of Silas M. Williams and his second wife Elizabeth Flett, Silas Leslie, was born in Nelson, Northumberland, New Brunswick, Canada on October 24, 1898.

When the 1921 Census of Canada was taken, Silas Leslie, then age twenty-three was recorded as working in Nelson and living with his widowed mother. His occupation was listed as a "journeyman blacksmith"

On September 6, 1928, Silas Leslie, who was traveling to Detroit, Wayne, Michigan to visit a friend, was recorded at the United States Detroit Border Crossing.

Sometime after he crossed the United States border on September 6, 1928 and the publishing of the 1935 Canada Voters Lists for the Electoral District of Nelson, Silas Leslie married Margaret Helena McCormick. The exact date and place of their marriage has not been found. Margaret Helena, the daughter of Fenton Stanislaus McCormick and Mary Agnes McLaughlin, was born in Blackville, Northumberland, New Brunswick on March 7, 1905.

Silas Leslie and Margaret Helena had two children during their marriage.

Jack	b.	d.
Elizabeth	b.	d.

From 1935 through 1968 the Canada Voters Lists for the Electoral District of Northumberland that included the Nelson area recorded Silas Leslie and Margaret Helena as living in South Nelson, Northumberland, New Brunswick. In those documents Silas Leslie's occupation was listed as "plumber".

Silas Leslie died, at the age of seventy-two, on November 4, 1970 at the Miramichi Hospital in Newcastle, Northumberland, New Brunswick. The cause of his death has not been found. His funeral, officiated by Reverend Sydney Snow, was held at St. James United Church in Nelson at 2:00 P.M. on Saturday, November 7, 1970. Silas Leslie was buried alongside his parents in the St. James United Cemetery in Nelson.

Margaret Helena outlived her husband by twenty-three years dying on May 6, 1993 at the age of eighty-eight at the Miramichi Hospital. The exact cause of her death has not been found. Her funeral was held at 11:00 A.M. on Saturday, May 8, 1993 at St. Patrick's Roman Catholic Church in Nelson with Father Leon Creamer presiding. She was buried that same day in the Malcolm Cemetery which is located next to St. Patrick's Roman Catholic Church. During her life Margaret Helena was a "school teacher" in the Nelson area.

SOURCES:

Silas Leslie Williams
Birth: Province of New Brunswick, Certificate of Registration of Birth, Northumberland Sub-Health District.
Death: (1) Record of Burial, Archives, Maritime Conference, The United Church of Canada, Sackville, Northumberland, New Brunswick, Canada; (2) Obituary, Miramichi Press, Wednesday November 11, 1970; (3) "Cemeteries of the Parish of Nelson, Northumberland County, Province of New Brunswick, Canada", Page 55, NB Genealogical Society-Miramichi Branch, 2002.
Graveyard: "Cemeteries of the Parish of Nelson, Northumberland County, Province of New Brunswick, Canada", Page 55, NB Genealogical Society-Miramichi Branch, 2002.

Margaret Helena McCormick
Birth: (1) Birth, Registration Division of Northumberland County, New Brunswick; (2) "Canada, Births and Baptisms, 1661-1959," database, FamilySearch (https://familysearch.org/ark:/61903/1.1:F28N-384).
Marriage:
Death: (1) Funeral Records, Bell's Funeral Home, Miramichi, Northumberland, New Brunswick, Canada; (2) Obituary, Miramichi Leader, Wednesday, May 12, 1993.
Graveyard: "Cemeteries of the Parish of Nelson, Northumberland County, Province of New Brunswick, Canada", Page 92, NB Genealogical Society-Miramichi Branch, 2002.

Historical Accounts: (1) 1921 Census of Canada, Nelson, Northumberland, New Brunswick, Page 9; (2) 1921 Census of Canada, Blackville, Northumberland, New Brunswick, Page 26; (3) Detroit Border Crossings and Passenger and Crew lists, 1905-1957, September 6, 1928; (4) Canada, Voter Lists, 1935 List of Electors, Electoral District of Northumberland, N.B., Rural Polling Division No. 39, Parish of Nelson, Page 2; (5) Canada, Voter Lists, 1945 Rural Preliminary List of Electors, Electoral District of Northumberland, Rural Polling Division No. 39, South Nelson, Page 3; (6) Canada, Voter Lists, 1949 Rural Preliminary List of Electors, Electoral District of Northumberland, Rural Polling Division No. 39, South Nelson, Page 3; (7) Canada, Voter Lists, 1953 Rural Preliminary List of Electors, Electoral District of Northumberland, Rural Polling Division No. 41, Page 2; (8) Canada, Voter Lists, 1962 Rural Preliminary List of Electors, Electoral District of Northumberland-Miramichi, Rural Polling Division No. 41, Page 3; (9) Canada, Voter Lists, 1968 Rural Preliminary List of Electors, Electoral District of Northumberland-Miramichi-South Nelson, Rural Polling Division No. 47, Page 2.

Frederick Willard Cusack

(1873 – 1956)

Frederick Willard was the first child of Eliza Ann Williams and Peter Cusack. He was born on September 15, 1873 in South Bay, Saint John, New Brunswick, Canada.

Frederick Willard Cusack
(Photograph Courtesy of Donald Emerson Smith and Donna Smith)

On April 20, 1914, at the age of forty, Frederick Willard was married to Mahala Thompson age twenty-eight in Fairville, Saint John, New Brunswick by Walter P. Dunham, Clergyman. Frederick Willard's sister, Minnie Loretta Cusack, and William John Morrison, the husband of his sister Mary Alice Cusack, were the official witnesses for the wedding. Mahala, the daughter of John Charles Thompson and his wife Anna, was born on May 2, 1886 in Derbyshire, England. Her exact place of birth has not been found. There is no record of Frederick Willard and Mahala ever having children.

In the 1921 Census of Canada Frederick Willard and Mahala were recorded as living on George Street in Fairville with Frederick Willard listed as working as a "laborer".

In 1945 Voter List of Canada for the Electoral District of Saint John-Albert Frederick Willard was listed as a "machinist" living in Milford, Saint John, New Brunswick.

Mahala died at the age of fifty-nine on January 15, 1946 at the Provincial Hospital in Fairville. Her cause of death was listed as "vascular disease of the heart". During her lifetime Mahala had also suffered from "schizophrenia" which was considered a contributing factor to her death. She was buried in

Section B, Grave 167at the Cedar Hill Extension Cemetery in Saint John West, Saint John, New Brunswick on January 18, 1945.

Frederick Willard outlived Mahala by more than eleven years dying of a "cerebral hemorrhage" at the age of eighty-three on October 16, 1956 at his home at 494 Milford Road, Lancaster, Saint John, New Brunswick. On October 18, 1856 he was buried alongside his wife at the Cedar Hill Extension Cemetery in Saint John West in Section B, Grave 166.

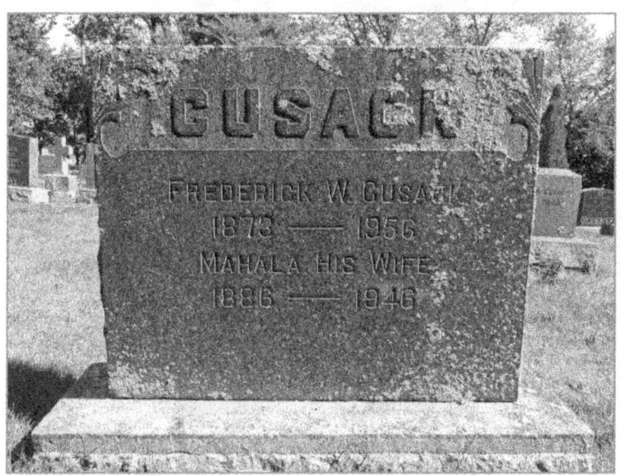

Gravestone for Frederick Willard Cusack and Mahala Thompson
(Photograph from the collection of Jeffrey N. Williams and Jacqueline Pon Williams)

SOURCES:

Frederick Willard Cusack
Birth: Province of New Brunswick - Registration of Death, Saint John City and County Sub-Health District.
Death: (1) Province of New Brunswick - Registration of Death, Saint John City and County Sub-Health District; (2) Brenan's Funeral Home Records, Saint John - Provincial Archives of New Brunswick.
Graveyard: (1) Listing of Interments prepared by Greenwood Cedar Hill Cemetery Company, Saint John West, Saint John, New Brunswick, September 2016; (2) Province of New Brunswick - Registration of Death, Saint John City and County Sub-Health District; (3) Brenan's Funeral Home Records, Saint John - Provincial Archives of New Brunswick.

Mahala Thompson
Birth: Province of New Brunswick - Registration of Death, Saint John City and County Sub-Health District.
Marriage: (1) Marriage, Registration Division of Saint John City and County, New Brunswick; (2) Acadia, Canada, Vital and Church Records (Drouin Collection), 1908-1919, Page 112.
Death: Province of New Brunswick - Registration of Death, Saint John City and County Sub-Health District.
Graveyard: (1) Listing of Interments prepared by Greenwood Cedar Hill Cemetery Company, Saint John West, Saint John, New Brunswick, September 2016; (2) Province of New Brunswick - Registration of Death, Saint John City and County Sub-Health District.

Historical Accounts: (1) 1891 Census of Canada, Lancaster, Saint John, New Brunswick, Page 24; (2) 1921 Census of Canada, Lancaster, Saint John, New Brunswick, Page 13; (3) Canada, Voter Lists, 1945 Rural Preliminary List of Voters, Electoral District of Saint John-Albert, Rural Polling Division No. 153, Parish of Lancaster, Page 1; (4) Genealogy Notes for Eliza Ann Williams, Peter Cusack and their children provided by Donald Emerson Smith and Donna Smith.

George Clifford Cusack

(1874 – 1953)

The second child of Eliza Ann Williams and Peter Cusack was George Clifford who was born on July 31, 1874 in South Bay, Saint John, New Brunswick, Canada.

George Clifford Cusack
(Photograph Courtesy of Donald Emerson Smith and Donna Smith)

At age sixteen, George Clifford was recorded as living with his parent in Lancaster, Saint John, New Brunswick when the 1891 Census of Canada was taken.

During his life George Clifford worked on tug boats as a "cook" in the Saint John County area. He also worked as a "fireman" on the steamer Fanchon in July 1894. From the records found it appears that he never married or had children.

At the age of seventy-eight George Clifford died of "pneumonia" on April 3, 1953 at his home at 28 Fallsview Avenue in Saint John City, Saint John, New Brunswick. He was buried with his sister, Mary Alice (Cusack) Morrison, and her family in the Morrison family plot, Lot 465, Avenue 10, at Old Cedar Hill Cemetery in Saint John West, Saint John, New Brunswick on April 6, 1958.

It should be noted here that the Morrison family plot at the Old Cedar Hill Cemetery in Saint John West contains no headstone for George Clifford Cusack, only single a marker with the Morrison family name.

Morrison Family Plot Marker, Old Cedar Hill Cemetery, Saint John West
(Photograph from the collection of Jeffrey N. Williams and Jacqueline Pon Williams)

SOURCES:

George Clifford Cusack
Birth: Certificate of Registration of Death, Province of New Brunswick.
Death: (1) Certificate of Registration of Death, Province of New Brunswick; (2) Brenan's Funeral Home Records, Saint John; Provincial Archives of New Brunswick.
Graveyard: (1) Listing of Interments prepared by Greenwood Cedar Hill Cemetery Company, September 2016, Saint John, New Brunswick; (2) Certificate of Registration of Death, Province of New Brunswick; (3) Brenan's Funeral Home Records, Saint John; Provincial Archives of New Brunswick.

Historical Accounts: (1) 1891 Census of Canada, Lancaster, Saint John, New Brunswick, Page 24: (2) Death Notice for Peter Cusack, "New Brunswick Vital Statistics from Newspapers", by Daniel F. Johnson, Volume 91, Number 1362, Provincial Archives of New Brunswick.

Mary Alice Cusack

(1875 – 1961)

Mary Alice, the third child of Eliza Ann Williams and Peter Cusack, was born in South Bay, Saint John, New Brunswick, Canada on November 8, 1875.

Mary Alice Cusack (left) and William John Morrison (right)
(Photographs Courtesy of Donald Emerson Smith and Donna Smith)

On November 14, 1894, at the age of nineteen, Mary Alice was married to William John Morrison age twenty-two in Fairville, Saint John, New Brunswick by William S. B. MacKiel. William John, born on March 4, 1871 in Fairville, was the son of John Morrison and Frances Elizabeth Cooper. At the time of his marriage William John was working as a "millman".

Mary Alice and William John had a large family of fourteen children.

Lauretta Marguerite	b. July 19, 1895	d. December 25, 1982
Edna Lyle	*b. February 21, 1897*	*d.*
Estelle Blanche	*b. June 24, 1898*	*d. February 21, 1899*
Hazel Irene	*b. February 17, 1900*	*d. March 23, 1920*
Alice Madeline	*b. January 14, 1902*	*d. May 18, 1902*
Gladys Muriel	b. July 9, 1903	d. March 28, 2002
Frances Winifred	b. June 3, 1905	d. September 12, 2000
William W.	*b. July 1906*	*d. September 8, 1906*
Kenneth Albert	b. 1908	d. December 29, 1984
Helen Grace	b. July 19, 1909	d. February 28, 1998
Mildred Esther	b. February 27, 1913	d. March 1, 2002
Dorothy Curren	*b. June 12, 1914*	*d. August 30, 1914*
Thelma Elizabeth	*b. April 16, 1918*	*d. September 18, 1918*
Marion Cusack	b. September 6, 1920	d. June 20, 2001

On February 21, 1899 Estelle Blanch, the third child of Mary Alice and William John died at the age of eight months at the family home in Fairville. Her cause of death was listed as "inflammation of the lungs". Additionally sometime prior to the taking of the 1901 Census of Canada, her younger sister Edna Lyle died at a place and of a cause unknown. The places of burial for both Edna Lyle and Estelle Blanche have not been found.

When the 1901 Census of Canada was taken Mary Alice, William John and their family were recorded as living in Lancaster, Saint John, New Brunswick with William John working as a "millman".

The fifth child of Mary Alice and William John, Alice Madeline, died on May 18, 1902 at the family home in Fairville of "convulsions" at the age of four months four days old. Her place of burial has not been found.

William W., the eighth child of Mary Alice and William John, died at the family home of "cholera infantum" on September 8, 1906 at the age of two months. The location of his burial is also not known.

In the 1911 Census of Canada Mary Alice and William John were recorded as living in Saint John City, Saint John, New Brunswick. William John's occupation was listed as "working in a saw mill".

Dorothy Curren, the twelfth child of Mary Alice and William John, died in Saint John County on August 30, 1914 at the age of two months eighteen days old of "cholera infantum". She was buried in the Morrison family plot at the Old Cedar Hill Cemetery in Saint John West, Saint John, New Brunswick in Lot 465, Avenue 10.

Two years later on September 18, 1918, also in Saint John County, the thirteenth child of Mary Alice and William John, Thelma Elizabeth, died of "gastritis" at the age of five months two days old at the family home at Prospect Point, Saint John, New Brunswick. On her "Return of a Death on Application for a Burial Permit" it indicated that she too was buried at the Old Cedar Hill Cemetery in Saint John West.

The fourth child of Mary Alice and William John, Hazel Irene, died at her parents' home in Prospect Point, Saint John, New Brunswick of "pulmonary tuberculosis" on March 23, 1920 at the age of twenty years old. She was buried in the Morrison family plot, Lot 465, Avenue 10, at Old Cedar Hill Cemetery in Saint John West on March 29, 1920.

When the 1921 Census of Canada was taken Mary Alice and William John were recorded as still living on Prospect Point Road in Saint John City and William John's occupation was again listed as "working in a sawmill".

William John died, at the age of sixty-one, on September 13, 1932 at his home at 10 Fallsview Avenue in Saint John City. His cause of death was recorded as "pulmonary tuberculosis". At the time of his death William John was working as a "lumber buyer". William John was buried in the Morrison family plot, Lot 465, Avenue 10, on September 15th at the Old Cedar Hill Cemetery in Saint John West.

In the 1945 Revised Urban List of Electors for the Electoral District of Saint John-Albert Mary Alice, a "widow", and her daughter Marion, a "stenographer", were recorded as living at 28 Fallsview Avenue in Saint John City.

When the 1953 Urban Preliminary List of Electors for the Electoral District of Saint John-Albert was published Mary Alice, a "widow", was still living at 28 Fallsview Avenue in Saint John City along with her son Kenneth Albert, a "C.P.R. trucker".

Mary Alice outlived her husband William John by twenty-eight years dying of "pneumonia" at the age of eighty-five on March 12, 1961 in her home at 28 Fallsview Avenue in Saint John City. She too was buried in the Morrison family plot, Lot 465, Avenue 10 at the Old Cedar Hill Cemetery in Saint John West.

It should be noted here that the Morrison family plot at the Old Cedar Hill Cemetery in Saint John West contains no individual or group headstone for Mary Alice, William John, Dorothy Curren, Thelma Elizabeth or Hazel Irene, only single a marker with the family name.

Morrison Family Plot Marker, Old Cedar Hill Cemetery, Saint John West
(Photograph from the collection of Jeffrey N. Williams and Jacqueline Pon Williams)

SOURCES:

Mary Alice Cusack
Birth: Province of New Brunswick - Registration of Death Department of Health and Social Services, Saint John City and County Sub-Health District.
Death: (1) Province of New Brunswick - Registration of Death Department of Health and Social Services, Saint John City and County Sub-Health District; (2) Brenan's Funeral Home Records, Saint John - Provincial Archives of New Brunswick.
Graveyard: (1) Listing of Interments prepared by Greenwood Cedar Hill Cemetery Company, Saint John West, Saint John, New Brunswick, September 2016; (2)) Province of New Brunswick - Registration of Death Department of Health and Social Services, Saint John City and County Sub-Health District; (3) Brenan's Funeral Home Records, Saint John - Provincial Archives of New Brunswick.

William John Morrison
Birth: Department of Health - New Brunswick, Certificate of Registration of Death, Saint John City and County Sub-Health District.
Marriage: (1) Marriages, Registration Division of Saint John City and County, New Brunswick; (2) Acadia, Canada, Vital and Church Records (Drouin Collection), 1888-1895, Page 81.
Death: Department of Health - New Brunswick, Certificate of Registration of Death, Saint John City and County Sub-Health District.
Graveyard: (1) Listing of Interments prepared by Greenwood Cedar Hill Cemetery Company, Saint John West, Saint John, New Brunswick, September 2016; (2) Department of Health - New Brunswick, Certificate of Registration of Death, Saint John City and County Sub-Health District.

Edna Lyle Morrison
Birth: (1) Office of Registrar, Births, Marriages, and Deaths, 222 Brittain Street, Saint John, N. B.; (2) Acadia, Canada, Vital and Church Records (Drouin Collection), 1893-1898, Schedule of Births, Page 133.
Death:
Graveyard:

Estelle Blanche Morrison
Birth: (1) Births, Registration Division of Saint John City and County, New Brunswick; (2) Acadia, Canada, Vital and Church Records (Drouin Collection), 1899-1905, Schedule of Births, Page 4; (3) Index to County Birth Registers, Microfilm F14956, Provincial Archives of New Brunswick.
Death: Deaths, Return of Clergyman, Occupier or Other Person, Registration Division of Saint John City and County, New Brunswick.
Graveyard:

Hazel Irene Morrison
Birth: "Canada, Births and Baptisms, 1661-1959," index, FamilySearch (https://familysearch.org/pal: /MM9.1.1 /F28P-MQ1).
Death: Department of Health - New Brunswick, Certificate of Registration of Death, Saint John City and County Sub-Health District.
Graveyard: (1) Listing of Interments prepared by Greenwood Cedar Hill Cemetery Company, Saint John West, Saint John, New Brunswick, September 2016; (2) Department of Health - New Brunswick, Certificate of Registration of Death, Saint John City and County Sub-Health District.

Alice Madeline Morrison
Birth: Births, Registration Division of Saint John City and County, New Brunswick.
Death: Deaths, Return of Clergyman, Occupier or Other Person, Registration Division of Saint John City and County, New Brunswick.
Graveyard:

William W. Morrison
Birth:
Death: Acadia, Canada, Vital and Church Records (Drouin Collection), 1901-1909, Schedule of Deaths, Page 116.
Graveyard:

Dorothy Curren Morrison
Birth: Births, Registration Division of Saint John City and County, New Brunswick.
Death: (1) Deaths, Registration Division of Saint John City and County, New Brunswick; (2) "New Brunswick, Saint John, Saint John, Burial Permits, 1889-1919," database with images, FamilySearch (https://familysearch. org/ark:/61903/1:1: Q2WK-GGWQ).
Graveyard: (1) Listing of Interments prepared by Greenwood Cedar Hill Cemetery Company, Saint John West, Saint John, New Brunswick, September 2016; (2) "New Brunswick, Saint John, Saint John, Burial Permits, 1889-1919," database with images, FamilySearch (https://familysearch. org/ark:/61903/1:1: Q2WK-GGWQ).

Thelma Elizabeth Morrison
Birth: Index to Provincial Registration of Births, Microfilm F25345, Provincial Archives of New Brunswick.
Death: (1) Deaths, Registration Division of Saint John City and County, New Brunswick; (2) "New Brunswick, Saint John, Saint John, Burial Permits, 1889-1919," database with images, FamilySearch (https://familysearch. org/ark:/61903/1:1: Q2WK-P3GT).
Graveyard: "New Brunswick, Saint John, Saint John, Burial Permits, 1889-1919," database with images, FamilySearch (https://familysearch. org/ark:/61903/1:1: Q2WK-P3GT).

Historical Accounts: (1) 1891 Census of Canada, Lancaster, Saint John, New Brunswick, Page 24; (2) 1901 Census of Canada, Lancaster, Saint John, New Brunswick, Page 38; (3) 1911 Census of Canada, Saint John, Saint John, New Brunswick, Page 24; (4) 1921 Census of Canada, Saint John, Saint John, New Brunswick, Page 3; (5) Canada, Voters List, 1945 Revised Urban List of Electors, Electoral District of Saint John-Albert, Urban Polling Division No. 1, Page 2; (6) Canada, Voters List, 1953 Urban Preliminary List of Electors, Electoral District of Saint John-Albert, Urban Polling Division No. 1, Page 2; (7) Genealogical history for Mary Alice Cusack and William John Morrison courtesy of Donald Emerson Smith and Donna Smith.

Minnie Loretta Cusack

(1877 – 1968)

The fourth child of Eliza Ann Williams and Peter Cusack, Minnie Loretta, was born on October 15, 1877 in South Bay, Saint John, New Brunswick, Canada.

Minnie Loretta was thirteen years old and living with her father Peter, a widower, in Lancaster, Saint John, New Brunswick when the 1891 Census of Canada was taken. Peter Cusack died two years later on July 4, 1894 after which the details of Minnie Loretta's life are unknown until 1916.

On June 30, 1916, at the age of thirty-eight, Minnie Loretta was married to Charles McEachern age thirty-four in Saint John City, Saint John, New Brunswick by Charles B. Appel. Minnie Loretta's niece, Lauretta Marguerite Morrison, and James McEachern, exact relationship unknown but presumed to be Charles' younger brother James Alexander, served as the official witnesses to the marriage. Charles, born on April 14, 1882 in Saint John County, was the son of John Duncan McEachern and Elizabeth Corrigan and was working as a "clerk" at the time of the wedding. There is no record of Minnie Loretta and Charles ever having children during their marriage.

In the 1921 Census of Canada Minnie Loretta and Charles were recorded as living at 549 Main Street in Dufferin Ward, Saint John, New Brunswick. Charles' occupation was listed as a "packer of dry goods".

At the age of forty eight, Charles died on April 28, 1930 in the General Public Hospital in Saint John City of an "intestinal obstruction". He was buried two days later, on April 30, 1930, in the McEachern family plot, Lot 565, Avenue 14, at the Old Cedar Hill Cemetery in Saint John West, Saint John, New Brunswick.

The 1945 Revised Urban List of Electors for the Electoral District of Saint John-Albert listed Minnie Loretta, a "widow", living at 89 Adelaide Street in Saint John City.

Minnie Loretta, at the age of ninety, died of a cause not known on January 14, 1968 in Saint John City at 50 Fallsview Avenue, the home of her niece Mildred Esther (Morrison) Crowe. Her funeral was held on Tuesday, January 16, 1968 at 3:00 P.M. Minnie Loretta was buried in the McEachern family plot, Lot 565, Avenue 14, at the Old Cedar Hill Cemetery in Saint John West.

It should be noted here that the McEachern family plot at the Old Cedar Hill Cemetery in Saint John West contains no individual or group headstone for Minnie Loretta and Charles, only single a marker with the family name.

McEachern Family Plot Marker, Old Cedar Hill Cemetery, Saint John West
(Photograph from the collection of Jeffrey N. Williams and Jacqueline Pon Williams)

SOURCES:

Minnie Loretta Cusack
Birth: (1) Province of New Brunswick, Department of Health, Certificate of Registration of Birth, Saint John City and County Sub-Health District; (2) Acadia, Canada, Vital and Church Records (Drouin Collection), 1888-1893, Schedule A – Births, Page 200; (3) "Canada, Births and Baptisms, 1661-1959," index, FamilySearch (https://familysearch.org/pal:MM9.1.1/F2HZ-8JQ).
Death: (1) Obituary, Evening Times Globe, Tuesday, January 16, 1968; (2) Listing of Interments prepared by Greenwood Cedar Hill Cemetery Company, Saint John West, Saint John, New Brunswick, September 2016.
Graveyard: Listing of Interments prepared by Greenwood Cedar Hill Cemetery Company, Saint John West, Saint John, New Brunswick, September 2016.

Charles McEachern
Birth: Department of Health - New Brunswick, Certificate of Registration of Death, Saint John City and County Sub-Health District.
Marriage: Marriage, Registration Division of Saint John City and County, New Brunswick.
Death: (1) Department of Health - New Brunswick, Certificate of Registration of Death, Saint John City and County Sub-Health District.; (2) Listing of Interments prepared by Greenwood Cedar Hill Cemetery Company, Saint John West, Saint John, New Brunswick, September 2016.
Graveyard: (1) Listing of Interments prepared by Greenwood Cedar Hill Cemetery Company, Saint John West, Saint John, New Brunswick, September 2016; (2) Department of Health - New Brunswick, Certificate of Registration of Death, Saint John City and County Sub-Health District.

Historical Accounts: (1) 1891 Census of Canada, Lancaster, Saint John, New Brunswick, Page 7; (2) 1921 Census of Canada, Dufferin Ward, Saint John, New Brunswick, Page 24; (3) Canada, Voters List, 1945 Revised Urban List of Electors, Electoral District of Saint John-Albert, Urban Polling Division No. 5, Page 1.

Arthur Welling Betts

(1873 – 1953)

Arthur Welling was the first child of Phoebe Elizabeth Williams and Wilford Welling Betts. He was born on November 6, 1873 in South Bay, Saint John, New Brunswick, Canada.

The 1891 Census of Canada recorded Arthur Welling, then age seventeen, as living with his parents in Lancaster, Saint John, New Brunswick and working as a "sawmill man".

At the age of twenty-two Arthur Welling was married to May Letitia McAuley, also age twenty-two, on July 22, 1896 by Reverend W. A. Sampson at the Rectory of St. George's Church in Carlton, Saint John, New Brunswick. Arthur Welling's brother, John Wilford Hartley Betts, and May Letitia's sister, Minnie McAuley, served as the official witnesses at their wedding. May Letitia, the daughter of Robert McAuley and Letitia Catherwood, was born on December 10, 1873 in Fairville, Saint John, New Brunswick.

Arthur Welling and May Letitia had one child together.

May Letitia	b. May 17, 1897	d. October 23, 1997

One day after the birth of their daughter, on May 18, 1897, May Letitia then age twenty-three died of "convulsions" at home in Fairville. Her place of burial is not known.

A little more than two years later, on November 29, 1899, Arthur Welling, age twenty-five, married his second wife, Helen Elizabeth Smith, age sixteen, at her father's house in Prince of Wales, Saint John, New Brunswick. F. W. M. Bacon was the officiant at their wedding. The daughter of Joseph and Mary Smith, Helen Elizabeth was born in Prince of Wales on July 13, 1883. At the time of their wedding Arthur Welling was working as a "lumberman".

Arthur Welling had an additional five children with his second wife Helen Elizabeth.

Gordon Welling	b. January 15, 1901	d. October 14, 1956
Florence Helena	*b. April 6, 1902*	*d. August 1, 1903*
Irene Tait	b. 1903	d. 1949
William Leonard	b. June 6, 1905	d. June 20, 1925
Joseph Arthur	b. January 29, 1907	d. July 7, 1972

When the 1901 Census of Canada was taken Arthur Welling and Helen Elizabeth were recorded as living with her parents in Musquash, Saint John, New Brunswick. Arthur Welling was then working as a "millman".

On August 1, 1903 Florence Helena, the second child of Arthur Welling and Helen Elizabeth, died of "whooping cough" at her parents' house in Fairville when she was fifteen months old. Her place of burial is also unknown.

In the 1921 Census of Canada Arthur Welling, Helen Elizabeth and their family had moved and were recorded as living at 32 Woodville Road, Beaconsfield, Saint John, New Brunswick. Arthur Welling's occupation listed as a "car inspector" in that census.

After working for the Canadian Pacific Railroad for 35 years as a "carman" Arthur Welling retired in 1939.

Arthur Welling died on September 3, 1953 at the age of seventy-nine at his home at 187 Tower Street, Saint John West in Saint John, New Brunswick after several months of illness. His official cause of death was listed as a "cerebral hemorrhage". During his life he was a "vestryman" of St. Jude's Anglican Church in Saint John West and an accomplished musician, being a charter member of St. Mary's Band and a member of the 3rd Regimental Artillery Band.

The funeral for Arthur Welling was held at St. Jude's Anglican Church on the following Tuesday, September 8th, at 2:00 P.M. His obituary indicated that he was interred in St. George's Cemetery in Saint John West.

A little over sixteen months later on January 18, 1955, Helen Elizabeth, then age seventy-one, died of "coronary arteriosclerosis" at the Saint John General Hospital in Saint John City, Saint John, New Brunswick. Her funeral was held on Thursday, January 20th at St. Jude's Anglican Church in Saint John West. Helen Elizabeth's death notice also indicated that she was also buried at St. George's Cemetery in Saint John West.

SOURCES:

Arthur Welling Betts
Birth: Province of New Brunswick - Registration of Death, Saint John City and County Sub-Health District.
Death: (1) Province of New Brunswick - Registration of Death, Saint John City and County Sub-Health District; (2) Obituary, Evening Times Globe, Friday, September 4, 1953, Page 9; (3) Brenan's Funeral Home Records, Saint John; Provincial Archives of New Brunswick.
Graveyard: Obituary, Evening Times Globe, Friday, September 4, 1953.

May Letitia McAuley
Birth:
Marriage: (1) Marriage, Registration Division of Saint John City and County, New Brunswick; (2) Acadia, Canada, Vital and Church Records (Drouin Collection), 1891-1907, Schedule B-Marriages, Page 31.
Death: Deaths, Return of Clergyman, Occupier or Other Person, Registration Division of Saint John City and County, New Brunswick.
Graveyard:

Helen Elizabeth Smith
Birth: Province of New Brunswick - Registration of Death, Saint John City and County Sub-Health District.
Marriage: (1) Marriage Certificate, Registration Division of Saint John City and County, New Brunswick; (2) Acadia, Canada, Vital and Church Records (Drouin Collection), 1891-1907, Schedule – B Marriages, Page 72.
Death: (1) Province of New Brunswick - Registration of Death, Saint John City and County Sub-Health District; (2) Death Notice, Evening Times Globe, Tuesday, January 18, 1955, Page 11; (3) Brenan's Funeral Home Records, Saint John; Provincial Archives of New Brunswick.
Graveyard: Obituary, Evening Times Globe, Tuesday, January 18, 1955.

Florence Helena Betts
Birth: Births, Registration Division of Saint John City and County, New Brunswick.
Death: Deaths, Return of Clergyman, Occupier or Other Person, Registration Division of Saint John City and County, New Brunswick.
Graveyard:

Historical Accounts: (1) 1881 Census of Canada, Lancaster, Saint John, New Brunswick, Page 57; (2) 1891 Census of Canada, Lancaster, Saint John, New Brunswick, Page 85; (3) 1891 Census of Canada, Lancaster, Saint John, New Brunswick, Page 112; (4) 1891 Census of Canada, Musquash, Saint John, New Brunswick, Page 7; (5) 1901 Census of Canada, Musquash, Saint John, New Brunswick, Page 3; (6) 1921 Census of Canada, Beaconsfield, Saint John, New Brunswick, Page 22; (7) Obituary for Arthur Welling Betts, Evening Times Globe, Friday, September 4, 1953.

John Wilford Hartley Betts

(1875 – 1950)

The second child, John Wilford Hartley, of Phoebe Elizabeth Williams and Wilford Welling Betts was born in South Bay, Saint John, New Brunswick, Canada on May 10, 1875.

In the 1901 Census of Canada John Wilford Hartley, age twenty-five, was recorded as working as a "millman" and living with his parents in the Lancaster, Saint John, New Brunswick.

On January 18 1904 at the age of twenty-eight John Wilford Hartley was married to Lillian Elizabeth Dunham, age twenty-five, by Reverend William S. B. McKiel in Fairville, Saint John, New Brunswick. William F. Dunham, Lillian Elizabeth's brother, served as one of the witnesses at the wedding. Born on October 20, 1878 in Lancaster, Lillian Elizabeth was the daughter of George Dunham and Mary Lockhart.

John Wilford Hartley and Lillian Elizabeth had two children together.

Florence Eveline	b. April 13, 1906	d. May 10, 1973
Percival Hannington	b. April 9, 1910	d. November 8, 1983

Lillian Elizabeth, at age thirty-three, died at home in Fairville on April 9, 1910 due to the effect of "child birth" after giving birth to her son Percival Hannington. Her funeral was held the following Monday, April 11th at 2:00 P.M. The place of her burial is unknown.

When the 1911 Census of Canada was taken John Wilford Hartley and his two children, Florence Eveline and Percival Hannington, were recorded as living with his parents in Lancaster.

On October 29, 1915 John Wilford Hartley enlisted in the 140th Overseas Battalion of the Canadian Expeditionary Force. In his "Attestation Paper" he was described as being 5' 6 3/4" tall, with a dark complexion, hazel eyes and black hair. And in his "Medical History" record he reported that he had "diphtheria" when he was around ten years old and in 1899 had contracted "typhoid fever". During his service in World War I he served in Great Britain, France and Belgium, having joined Princess Patricia's Light Infantry in the field. He was "struck off service" on May 16, 1919 holding the rank of Sergeant.

On October 22, 1919, at the age of forty-four, John Wilford Hartley was married to his second wife in Fairville, the widow Helen Lyon (Ritchie) Jack age twenty-six, by Wallace P. Dunham, Clergyman. Helen Lyon, the daughter of Thomas I. Ritchie and Agnes Lyon, was born on May 19, 1893 at 63

Bellville Street in Greenock, Renfrewshire, Scotland. There is no record of John Wilford Hartley and Helen Lyon having any children together during their marriage, although Helen Lyon did have two children from her previous marriage.

Helen Lyon is believed to have died shortly after her marriage to John Wilford Hartley. No record of her death, place of burial or additional information regarding her life has been found.

At age fifty-one John Wilford Hartley was married to his third wife on April 20, 1927, the widow Sarah Matilda (Hurst) Finley, age fifty-nine, in the Church of the Good Shepard in Fairville by F. T. Leroy. Sarah Matilda, born in Carlton, Saint John, New Brunswick in 1868, was the daughter of William Hurst and Mary Ann Buchanan.

John Wilford Hartley and Sarah Matilda were recorded crossing the Canadian/United States border at Vanceboro, Washington, Maine on January 27, 1945. They were on their way to visit Alden E. Finley, Sarah Matilda's son from a prior marriage, in Kittery Point, York, Maine. In that manifest John Wilford Hartley was described as having a deformed right hand and blindness in his left eye.

On March 6, 1950 John Wilford Hartley, age seventy-four, died at the Lancaster Military Hospital in Lancaster of a "cerebral accident". He was buried at the Old Cedar Hill Cemetery in Saint John West, Saint John, New Brunswick in Lot 614 W1/2 on Avenue 16.

Gravestone for John Wilford Hartley Betts
(Photograph from the collection of Jeffrey N. Williams and Jacqueline Pon Williams)

Additional information regarding the life and death of John Wilford Hartley's third wife Sarah Matilda has not been found.

SOURCES:

John Wilfred Hartley Betts
Birth: Late Registration of Birth, Province of New Brunswick, Canada..
Death: (1) Province of New Brunswick - Certificate of Registration of Death, Saint John City and County Sub-Health District; (2) Brenan's Funeral Home Records, Saint John; Provincial Archives of New Brunswick.
Graveyard: (1) Listing of Interments prepared by Greenwood Cedar Hill Cemetery Company, Saint John West, Saint John, New Brunswick, September 2016; (2) Brenan's Funeral Home Records, Saint John; Provincial Archives of New Brunswick; (3) Province of New Brunswick - Certificate of Registration of Death, Saint John City and County Sub-Health District; (4) Find A Grave Memorial #172095816.

Lillian Elizabeth Dunham
Birth:
Marriage: (1) Marriage, Registration Division of Saint John City and County, New Brunswick; (2) Acadia, Canada, Vital and Church Records (Drouin Collection), 1891-1907, Schedule B – Marriages, Page 124.
Death: (1) Death Certificate, Registration Division of Saint John City and County, New Brunswick; (2) Obituary, Daily Telegraph, Monday, April 11, 1910, Page 2; (3) Death Notice, Daily Telegraph, Monday, April 11, 1910, Page 5.
Graveyard:

Helen Lyon Ritchie
Birth: Birth Record, 1893 Births in East District of Greenock, Renfrewshire, Scotland.
Marriage: Marriage Return, Registration Division of Saint John City and County, New Brunswick.
Death:
Graveyard:

Sarah Matilda Hurst
Birth:
Marriage: Province of New Brunswick, Department of Health, Official Notice of Marriage, Saint John City and County Sub-Health District.
Death:
Graveyard:

Historical Accounts: (1) 1901 Census of Canada, Lancaster, Saint John, New Brunswick, Page 32; (2) 1901 Census of Canada, Lancaster, Saint John, New Brunswick, Page 49; (3) John Wilford Betts, Canadian Expeditionary Records, Library and Archives of Canada, RG 150, Accession 1992-93/166, Box 708-10; (4) "Princess Patricia's Canadian Light Infantry 1914-1919"; by Ralph Hodder-Williams, Page 110, London Hodder and Stoughton, 1923; (5) "Vermont, St. Albans Canadian Border crossings, 1895-1954," database with images, FamilySearch (https://familysearch.org/ark:/61903/1:1:QK3R-TXBW: 9 October 2015)

Adelaide Winnifred Betts

(1878 – 1901)

Adelaide Winnifred, the third child of Phoebe Elizabeth Williams and Wilford Welling Betts was born in February 1878 in Grand Bay, Saint John, New Brunswick, Canada.

At the age of twenty-two Adelaide Winnifred was married to Robert John White age twenty-four by J. B. Daggett at Charles W. Betts' (relationship unknown) home in Pembroke, Carlton, New Brunswick on December 25, 1900. Robert John, the son of Robert White and Mary Davis, was born on February 7, 1876 in Milford, Saint John, New Brunswick. He was working as a "millman" at the time of his marriage to Adelaide Winnifred.

Adelaide Winnifred and Robert John had just one child.

John *b. December 2, 1901* *d. 1901*

On December 5, 1901 Adelaide Winnifred, age twenty-three, died at her home in Milford from complications of "child birth". As no record could be found regarding her son John's life it is presumed that he died around that time as well. Adelaide Winnifred was buried in the Betts family plot, Lot 46, Avenue E, at the St. George's Cemetery in Saint John West, Saint John, New Brunswick.

Headstone for Adelaide Winnifred Betts
(Photograph from the collection of Jeffrey N. Williams and Jacqueline Pon Williams

On December 2, 1903 Robert John, age twenty-seven, was married to his second wife the widow Fanny Laurine (McCutcheon) Tiner, age thirty-two, by A. T. Dykeman in Fairville, Saint John, New Brunswick. Fanny Laurine the daughter of John McCutcheon and Elizabeth Hamilton was born on September 25, 1871 in Hamilton Mountain, Queens, New Brunswick. No record has been found to indicate that Robert John and Fanny Laurine had any children together. However, she did have a son from her first marriage.

The 1911 Census of Canada recorded Robert John, Fanny Laurine and her son from her first marriage, Gray Redvers Tiner, living in Hamilton Mountain. Robert John was listed as working as a "farmer" in that census.

Robert John, Fanny Laurine and her son from her first marriage, Gray Redvers Tiner were living on and working their family farm in Petersville, Queens, New Brunswick when the 1921 Census of Canada was taken.

After forty-four years of marriage, Fannie Laurine died on May 6, 1948 in the Saint John General Hospital in Saint John City, Saint John, New Brunswick at the age of seventy-six. The cause of her death was recorded as "post-operative shock from surgery for cancer of the bowel". She was buried in the Browns Flat Baptist Cemetery at Browns Flat, Kings, New Brunswick.

During his life Robert John also worked as a "supervisor for highways" in the Province of New Brunswick. He lived for a little less than four years after his second wife passed, dying at the age of seventy-six from a "cerebral hemorrhage" on February 29, 1952 in Public Landing, Kings, New Brunswick. Robert John was also buried in the Browns Flat Baptist Cemetery at Browns Flat.

SOURCES:

Adelaide Winnifred Betts
Birth:
Death: (1) Deaths, Return of Clergyman, Occupier or Other Person, Registration Division of Saint John City and County, New Brunswick; (2) Death Notice, Saint John Gazette, December 5, 1901, Page 8.
Graveyard: Listing of Interments prepared by Greenwood Cedar Hill Cemetery Company, Saint John West, Saint John, New Brunswick, November 2012.

Robert John White
Birth: Province of New Brunswick - Registration of Death, Saint John City and County Sub-Health District.
Marriage: (1) Marriage, Registration Division of Carleton County, New Brunswick; (2) Arcadia, Canada, Vital and Church Records (Drouin Collection), 1888-1920, Schedule B – Marriages, Page 58.
Death: Province of New Brunswick - Registration of Death, Saint John City and County Sub-Health District.
Graveyard: (1) Brenan's Funeral Home Records, Saint John, Provincial Archives of New Brunswick ; (2) Province of New Brunswick - Certificate of Registration of Death, Saint John City and County Sub-Health District.

John White
Birth: Births, Registration Division of Saint John City and County, New Brunswick.
Death:
Graveyard:

Fannie Laurine McCutcheon
Birth: Province of New Brunswick - Certificate of Registration of Death, Saint John City and County Sub-Health District.
Marriage: Marriage, Registration Division of Carleton County, New Brunswick.
Death: Province of New Brunswick - Certificate of Registration of Death, Saint John City and County Sub-Health District.
Graveyard: (1) Brenan's Funeral Home Records, Saint John, Provincial Archives of New Brunswick ; (2) Province of New Brunswick - Certificate of Registration of Death, Saint John City and County Sub-Health District.

Historical Accounts: (1) 1891 Census of Canada, Parish of Lancaster, Saint John, New Brunswick, Page 112; (2) 1911 Census of Canada, Parish of Petersville, Queens, New Brunswick, Page 1; (3) 1921 Census of Canada, Petersville, Queens, New Brunswick, Page 19.

Percival Nelson Hannington Betts

(1882 – 1962)

The fifth child of Phoebe Elizabeth Williams and Wilford Welling, Percival Nelson Hannington, was born on December 14, 1882 in Fairville, Saint John, New Brunswick, Canada.

The 1901 Census of Canada recorded Percival Nelson Hannington at age eighteen living with his parents in Lancaster, Saint John, New Brunswick and working as a "blacksmith".

On December 23, 1908 Percival Nelson Hannington, age twenty-six, was married to Beula Maude Shaw, age twenty-five, by Reverend G. C. Jenkins in Carleton County, New Brunswick. Beula Maude, born on December 9, 1883 in Pembroke, Carleton, New Brunswick, was the daughter of George Whitfield Shaw and Etha Adelaide Grey.

During their marriage Percival Nelson Hannington and Beula Maude had three children.

Ivan Grenfell	b. August 25, 1912	d. June 14, 1985
Neta Aileen	b. October 30, 1914	d. October 14, 2014
Muriel Shaw	b. February 16, 1916	d. December 26, 1993

When the 1911 and 1921 Census' of Canada were taken Percival Nelson Hannington, Beula Maude their children had moved to Woodstock, Carleton, New Brunswick. Percival Nelson recorded as was working as a "blacksmith".

In the 1957 Rural Preliminary List of Electors for the Electoral District of Victoria-Carlton, Percival Nelson Hannington, a "laborer", and Beula Maude were recorded as still living in Woodstock.

Percival Nelson Hannington died at the Carleton Memorial Hospital in Woodstock of "carcinoma of the colon" on November 10, 1962 at the age of seventy-nine. He was buried in the Grafton Cemetery in Grafton, Carleton, New Brunswick.

When the 1963 Rural Preliminary List of Electors for the Electoral District of Victoria-Carlton was published Beula Maude, a "widow", was living on Broadway Street in Woodstock.

Beula Maude outlived her husband Percival Nelson Hannington by ten years dying in 1972 at the age of eighty-eight. The exact date, place and cause of her death are unknown. She too was buried in the Grafton Cemetery in Grafton.

Gravestone for Percival Nelson Hannington Betts and Beula Maude Shaw
(Photograph Courtesy of Dale and Patti, Find A Grave)

SOURCES:

Percival Nelson Hannington Betts
Birth: Province of New Brunswick - Registration of Death, Department of Health and Social Services, Carleton Sub-Health District.
Death: Province of New Brunswick - Registration of Death, Department of Health and Social Services, Carleton Sub-Health District.
Graveyard: (1) Province of New Brunswick - Registration of Death, Department of Health and Social Services, Carleton Sub-Health District; (2) Find A Grave, Memorial #101540320.

Beula Maude Shaw
Birth: Certificate of Registration of Birth, Province of New Brunswick.
Marriage: (1) Marriage, Registration Division of Carleton County, New Brunswick; (2) Acadia, Canada, Vital and Church Records (Drouin Collection), 1888-1920, Schedule B – Marriages, Page 103.
Death:
Graveyard: Find A Grave, Memorial #101540329.

Historical Accounts: (1) 1901 Census of Canada, Parish of Northampton, Carleton, New Brunswick, Page 7; (2) 1901 Census of Canada, Lancaster, Saint John, New Brunswick, Page 32; (3) 1911 Census of Canada, Woodstock, Carleton, New Brunswick, Page 4; (4) 1921 Census of Canada, Woodstock, Carleton, New Brunswick, Page 11; (5) Canada, Voters Lists - 1957 Rural Preliminary List of Electors, Electoral District of Victoria-Carlton, Rural Polling Division No. 54, Grafton, Page 1; (6) Canada, Voters Lists - 1963 Rural Preliminary List of Electors, Electoral District of Victoria-Carlton, Rural Polling Division No. 33, Town of Woodstock, Page 1.

Charles Clinton Betts

(1885 – 1949)

Charles Clinton was the sixth child of Phoebe Elizabeth Williams and Wilford Welling Betts. He was born in October 13, 1885 in Randolph, Saint John, New Brunswick, Canada.

The 1911 Census of Canada recorded Charles Clinton living with his parents in Lancaster, Saint John, New Brunswick.

On April 25, 1918 Charles Clinton was drafted into the 1st Depot Battalion, New Brunswick Regiment of the Canadian Army. In his military records he was described as being 5' 5½" tall, with hazel eyes, black hair and a medium complexion. At the time he was drafted Charles Clinton was living at home with his parents in Lancaster and working as a "musician". A little over a year later, on May 15, 1919, he was discharged from the Canadian Army holding the rank of Private.

Charles Clinton was recorded as crossing the border into the United States on May 10, 1920 for a one week visit to Brooklyn, Kings, New York. His occupation at that time was listed as "steam fitter". On October 10, 1922 he again crossed the border into the United States to visit his Uncle Wellington Betts in Cambridge, Middlesex, Massachusetts.

In the 1921 Census of Canada Charles Clinton was recorded as living with his father on George Street in Fairville, Saint John, New Brunswick. In that census Charles Clinton was listed as still working as a "steam fitter".

At the age of thirty-nine, on June 24, 1925, Charles Clinton was married to Hazel Maud Lillian King age twenty-eight, by Reverend Hazen F. Rigby at her father's home in Woodstock, Carleton, New Brunswick. Hazel Maud Lillian, the daughter of William R. King and Eliza Davis, was born in Woodstock on May 4, 1897. Her parents also served as the official witnesses at the wedding.

Charles Clinton and Hazel Maud Lillian's Official Notice of Marriage indicated that at the time of their marriage Charles Clinton was living in the State of New York and working in "plumbing and heating in the building trade". No record has been found to indicate that of Charles Clinton and Hazel Maud Lillian ever had children.

The 1940 Rural Preliminary List of Electors for the Electoral District of Saint John-Albert listed Charles Clinton, a "plumber", and Hazel Maud Lillian as living in Lancaster.

On June 1, 1949 Charles Clinton, a "plumber", and Hazel Maud Lillian were recorded as living at 229 Simms Street in Lancaster when the 1949 Rural

Preliminary List of Electors for the Electoral District of Saint John-Albert was published.

Charles Clinton died at the age of sixty-three on September 28, 1949 at his home at 229 Simms Street in Lancaster as a result of a "hemorrhage from a ruptured aorta". Charles Clinton was buried in the Church of the Good Shepherd Cemetery in Saint John West, Saint John, New Brunswick.

Hazel Maud Lillian outlived her husband by fourteen years, dying on April 4, 1963 at the home of George C. Chittick in Lancaster when she was sixty-five years old. The exact cause of her death is not known. Hazel Maud Lillian's funeral was held at 4:00 P.M. on Saturday, April 6th at the Calvin Funeral Home in Lancaster. She too was buried in the Church of the Good Shepherd Cemetery in Saint John West.

Gravestone for Charles Clinton Betts and Hazel Maud Lillian King
(Photograph from the collection of Jeffrey N. Williams and Jacqueline Pon Williams)

SOURCES:

Charles Clinton Betts
Birth: Department of Health - New Brunswick, Certificate of Registration of Death, Saint John City and County Sub-Health District.
Death: (1) Department of Health - New Brunswick, Certificate of Registration of Death, Saint John City and County Sub-Health District; (2) Brenan's Funeral Home Records, Saint John; Provincial Archives of New Brunswick.
Graveyard: (1) Listing of Interments prepared by Greenwood Cedar Hill Cemetery Company, Saint John West, Saint John, New Brunswick, September 2016; (2) Department of Health - New Brunswick, Certificate of Registration of Death, Saint John City and County Sub-Health District; (3) Find A Grave, Memorial #129248525.

Hazel Maud Lillian King
Birth: (1) Birth, Registration Division of Carleton County, New Brunswick; (2) Index to County Birth Registers, Microfilm F14030, Provincial Archives of New Brunswick.
Marriage: Province of New Brunswick, Department of Health, Official Notice of Marriage, Carleton Sub-Health District.
Death: (1) Death Notice, Evening Times Globe, Saturday, April 6, 1963, Page 17; (2) Listing of Interments prepared by Greenwood Cedar Hill Cemetery Company, Saint John West, Saint John, New Brunswick, September 2016.
Graveyard: (1) Listing of Interments prepared by Greenwood Cedar Hill Cemetery Company, Saint John West, Saint John, New Brunswick, September 2016; (2) Find A Grave, Memorial #129248539.

Historical Accounts: (1) 1911 Census of Canada, Woodstock, Carleton, New Brunswick, Page 32; (2) 1921 Census of Canada, Lancaster, Saint John, New Brunswick, Page 13; (3) Charles Betts, Canadian Expeditionary Records, Library and Archives of Canada, RG 150, Accession 1992-93/166, Box 707-32; (4) Border Crossings from Canada to the U. S., 1895-1959; (5) U. S. Records of Aliens Pre-Examined in Canada 1917-1954; (6) Canada, Voters Lists - 1940 Rural Preliminary List of Electors, Electoral District of Saint John-Albert, Rural Polling Division No. 143 Lancaster, Page 1; (7) Canada, Voters Lists - 1949 Rural Preliminary List of Electors, Electoral District of Saint John-Albert, Rural Polling Division No. 167, Beaconsfield, Page 1.

James Franklin Williams

(1877 – 1935)

The first child of Benjamin Franklin Williams and Jane Brown was James Franklin (commonly known as Frank). He was born in Lancaster, Saint John, New Brunswick, Canada on September 5, 1877.

When the 1901 Census of Canada was taken, James Franklin then age twenty-two was recorded as living with his parents in Lancaster, Saint John, New Brunswick and working as a "millman".

On June 8, 1904 James Franklin, age twenty-six, was married to Beatrice Maud Ogden age twenty-four, by A. C. Bell in the Hall at Clarendon Station, Queens, New Brunswick. The official witnesses for their wedding were James Franklin's sister Estella Williams and Beatrice Maud's brother Edward S. Ogden. Beatrice Maud, born on January 6, 1880 in Clarendon Station, was the daughter of William Henry Ogden and Susannah A. Nickerson.

James Franklin and Beatrice Maud had six children.

Audrey Pearl	b. June 23, 1905	d. December 10, 1982
Benjamin Henry	b. February 26, 1907	d. May 14, 1971
Eldora Madeline	b. February 1, 1909	d. November 14, 1992
Gilbert Franklin	b. September 30, 1911	d. September 2, 1989
Harold Peter	b. July 8, 1923	d. April 15, 1998
Ethel	*b.*	*d.*

In the 1911 Census of Canada James Franklin, Beatrice Maud and their family were recorded as living in Clarendon Station. James Franklin was then working as a "laborer".

By the time the 1921 Census of Canada was taken James Franklin and Beatrice Maud had moved their family to 153 Brussels Street, Wellington Ward, Saint John, New Brunswick. James Franklin's occupation was recorded as an "edge man" in a factory.

James Franklin, at age fifty-seven, died at the Saint John General Hospital in Saint John City, Saint John, New Brunswick on July 13, 1935 of "carcinoma of the liver". His death certificate indicated that he had been working as a "longshoreman" until April of that year. James Franklin was buried in his father Benjamin Franklin Williams' plot at the Old Cedar Hill Cemetery, Avenue 49, Lot 295, in Saint John West, Saint John, New Brunswick on July 15, 1935. There is no headstone marking his grave.

In the 1940 Rural Preliminary List of Electors for the Electoral District of Saint John-Albert, Beatrice Maud was recorded as living with her son Gilbert

Franklin and his wife on River Avenue in the Parish of Simonds in East Saint John, Saint John, New Brunswick

Beatrice Maud moved to Montreal, Quebec, Canada sometime between February 14, 1940, when the 1940 Rural Preliminary List of Electors for the Electoral District of Saint John-Albert was published, and February 17, 1958, when the 1958 Urban List of Electors for the City of Montreal was published. In the 1958 Urban List of Electors she was listed as living with her daughter Audrey Pearl (Williams) McAinsh in Montreal at 5858 Sherbrooke Street West, Apartment 19.

By the time the 1962 Urban List of Electors was published on May 8, 1962 Beatrice Maud's daughter Audrey Pearl had married her second husband, Joseph Brendon Crinion. In that document Beatrice Maud was listed as living with them at the 5858 Sherbrooke Street West, Apartment 19 address in Montreal.

Beatrice Maud outlived her husband by almost twenty-eight years dying at the age of eighty-three on June 8, 1963 at the Montreal Metropolitan Hospital in Montreal, Quebec, Canada. The cause of her death has not been found. Her body was shipped by train to Saint John City for her funeral and interment. Beatrice Maud was buried at the Cedar Hill Extension Cemetery in Saint John West in Section F, Grave 344.

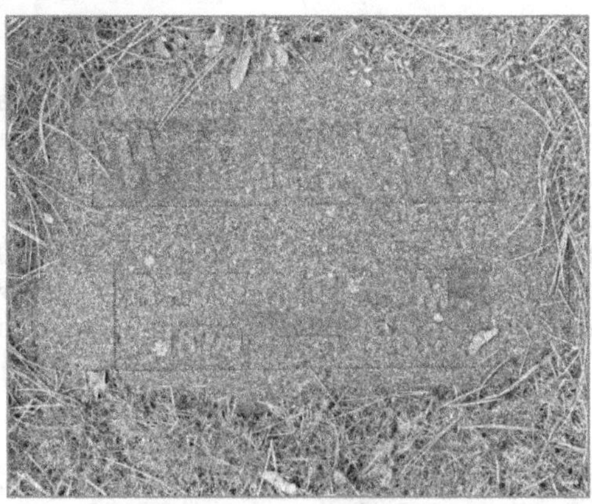

Headstone for Beatrice Maud Ogden
(Photograph from the collection of Jeffrey N. Williams and Jacqueline Pon Williams)

In Beatrice Maud's death notice it indicated that she was survived by a daughter Ethel. Additional information regarding the birth, marriage or death of Ethel has not been found.

SOURCES:

James Franklin Williams
Birth: Province of New Brunswick - Certificate of Registration of Death, Saint John City and County Sub-Health District.
Death: Province of New Brunswick - Certificate of Registration of Death, Saint John City and County Sub-Health District.
Graveyard: (1) Listing of Interments prepared by Greenwood Cedar Hill Cemetery Company, Saint John West, Saint John, New Brunswick, November 2012; (2) Province of New Brunswick - Certificate of Registration of Death, Saint John City and County Sub-Health District.

Beatrice Maud Ogden
Birth: 1901 Census of Canada, Parish of Petersville, Queens, New Brunswick, Page 15.
Marriage: (1) Marriage, Registration District of Queens County, New Brunswick; (2) Acadia, Canada, Vital and Church Records (Drouin Collection), Queens, 1888-1919, Schedule B – Marriages, Page 27.
Death: (1) Death Notice, The Montreal Star, Monday June 16, 1963, Page 16; (2) Death Notice, Evening Times Globe, Monday, June 10, 1963, Page 17; (3) Listing of Interments prepared by Greenwood Cedar Hill Cemetery Company, Saint John West, Saint John, New Brunswick, November 2012.
Graveyard: Listing of Interments prepared by Greenwood Cedar Hill Cemetery Company, Saint John West, Saint John, New Brunswick, November 2012.

Historical Accounts: (1) 1901 Census of Canada, Parish of Petersville, Queens, New Brunswick, Page 15; (2) 1901 Census of Canada, Lancaster, Saint John, New Brunswick, Page 10; (3) 1911 Census of Canada, Parish of Petersville, Queens, New Brunswick, Pages 20 & 21; (4) 1921 Census of Canada, Wellington Ward, Saint John, New Brunswick, Page 11; (5) Canada, Voter Lists, 1940 Rural Preliminary List of Voters, Electoral District of Saint John-Albert, Rural Polling Division No. 134B, Parish of Simonds, Page 2; (6) Canada, Voter Lists, 1958 Urban Preliminary List of Electors, Electoral District of Notre Dame de Grace, City of Montreal, Urban Polling Division No. 138, Page 2; (7) Canada, Voter Lists, 1962 Urban Preliminary List of Electors, Electoral District of Notre Dame de Grace, City of Montreal, Urban Polling Division No. 218, Page 2.

Olive Edna Williams

(1879 – 1951)

Olive Edna, the second child of Benjamin Franklin Williams and Jane Brown, was born on October 30, 1879 in St. Martins, Saint John, New Brunswick, Canada.

The 1901 Census of Canada recorded Olive Edna as living with her parents in Lancaster, Saint John, New Brunswick and working as a "dressmaker".

On October 22, 1902 at the age of twenty-two Olive Edna was married to Frank Ernest Ring, age twenty-one, at Milford, Saint John, New Brunswick by A. T. Dykeman. Olive Edna's brother James Franklin Williams and her sister Estella Williams served as the official witnesses at the wedding. Frank Ernest, a "stevedore" by trade, was the son of Everett Jeremiah Ring and Malvina Jane Gough. He was born on June 20, 1880 in Carleton, Saint John, New Brunswick. There is no record of Olive Edna and Frank Ernest ever having children during their marriage.

When the 1911 Census of Canada Charles, was taken Olive Edna and Frank Ernest were recorded as living at 7 Germain Street in Brooks Ward, Saint John City, Saint John, New Brunswick. Frank Ernest was listed as working as a "ship laborer" in that census.

In the 1921 Census of Canada Olive Edna and Frank Ernest had moved to 109 Queen Street in Brooks Ward. In that census Frank Ernest's occupation was listed as a "laborer".

The 1949 Canada Voter List for the Electoral District of Saint John-Albert recorded Olive Edna, a "housewife", and Frank Ernest, a "fisherman", as still living at 109 Queen Street in Brooks Ward.

On March 21, 1951 Olive Edna died at her home on Queen Street in Brooks Ward at the age of seventy-one. Her cause of death was recorded as "coronary heart disease". She was buried in Section C, Lot 84 A W1/2 at the Cedar Hill Extension Cemetery in Saint John West, Saint John, New Brunswick on March 23, 1951.

When the 1957 Canada Voter List for the Electoral District of Saint John-Albert was published Frank Ernest was listed as being retired and living at 155 Ludlow Street in Saint John West.

Frank Ernest died, at the age of eighty-seven, on August 2, 1967 at the Saint John General Hospital in Saint John City. The cause of his death has not been found. His funeral was held at 2:00 P.M. on Friday, August 4, 1967 at the

Calvin Funeral Home in Saint John West. Frank Ernest was also buried in Section C, Lot 84 A W1/2 at the Cedar Hill Extension Cemetery in Saint John West alongside his wife.

Gravestone for Olive Edna Williams and Frank Ernest Ring
(Photograph from the collection of Jeffrey N. Williams and Jacqueline Pon Williams)

SOURCES:

Olive Edna Williams
Birth: (1) Certificate of Registration of Birth, Province of New Brunswick; (2) Index to Late Registration of Births: Microfilm F18766, Provincial Archives of New Brunswick.
Death: (1) Province of New Brunswick - Certificate of Registration of Death, Saint John City and County Sub-Health District; (2) Listing of Interments prepared by Greenwood Cedar Hill Cemetery Company, Saint John West, Saint John, New Brunswick, September 2016.
Graveyard: (1) Listing of Interments prepared by Greenwood Cedar Hill Cemetery Company, Saint John West, Saint John, New Brunswick, September 2016; (2) Province of New Brunswick - Certificate of Registration of Death, Saint John City and County Sub-Health District.

Frank Ernest Ring
Birth: Certificate of Registration of Birth, Province of New Brunswick.
Marriage: Marriage, Registration Division of Saint John City and County, New Brunswick.
Death: (1) Death Notice, Evening Times Globe, Wednesday, August 2, 1967, Page 28; (2) Listing of Interments prepared by Greenwood Cedar Hill Cemetery Company, Saint John West, Saint John, New Brunswick, September 2016.
Graveyard: Listing of Interments prepared by Greenwood Cedar Hill Cemetery Company, Saint John West, Saint John, New Brunswick, September 2016.

Historical Accounts: (1) 1901 Census of Canada, Parish of Lancaster, Saint John, New Brunswick, Page 10; (2) 1901 Census of Canada, Brooks Ward, Saint John, New Brunswick, Page 3; (3) 1911 Census of Canada, Brooks Ward, Saint John, New Brunswick, Page 33; (4) 1921 Census of Canada, Brooks Ward, Saint John, New Brunswick, Page 18; (5) 1949 Canada Voter List for the Electoral District of Saint John-Albert, Urban Polling Division 124, Page 1; (6) 1957 Canada Voter List for the Electoral District of Saint John-Albert, Urban Polling Division 133, Page 2.

John Garnett Williams

(1882 – 1937)

The third child, John Garnett (also known as Garnett), of Benjamin Franklin Williams and Jane Brown was born in South Bay, Saint John, New Brunswick, Canada on May 20, 1882.

The 1901, 1911 and 1921 Census' of Canada recorded John Garnett as living with his parents in Lancaster, Saint John, New Brunswick and working as a "laborer".

During his lifetime no records have been found to indicate that John Garnett had ever married or had any children.

John Garnett died at the age of fifty-seven on February 17, 1937 at the Saint John General Hospital in Saint John City, Saint John, New Brunswick. His cause of death was recorded as "peritonitis as a result of a perforated gastric ulcer". John Garnett had been working as a "laborer" until February 15th of that year. At the time of his death he was still living with his parents at 39 Havelock Street in Lancaster. He was buried in the Old Cedar Hill Cemetery in Saint John West, Saint John, New Brunswick on February 19, 1937 in his father Benjamin Franklin Williams' plot at Avenue 49, Lot 295. There is no headstone marking his grave.

SOURCES:

John Garnett Williams
Birth: Province of New Brunswick - Certificate of Registration of Death, Saint John City and County Sub-Health District.
Death: Province of New Brunswick - Certificate of Registration of Death, Saint John City and County Sub-Health District.
Graveyard: (1) Listing of Interments prepared by Greenwood Cedar Hill Cemetery Company, Saint John West, Saint John, New Brunswick, November 2012; (2) Province of New Brunswick - Certificate of Registration of Death, Saint John City and County Sub-Health District.

Historical Accounts: (1) 1901 Census of Canada, Parish of Lancaster, Saint John, New Brunswick, Page 10; (2) 1911 Census of Canada, Parish of Lancaster, Saint John, New Brunswick, Page 23; (3) 1921 Census of Canada, Parish of Lancaster, Saint John, New Brunswick, Page 23.

Estella Williams

(1884 – 1973)

Estella (commonly known as Stella) was the fourth child of Benjamin Franklin Williams and Jane Brown. She was born on September 7, 1884 in South Bay, Saint John, New Brunswick, Canada.

In the 1901 Census of Canada Estella, then sixteen years old, was recorded as living with her parents in Lancaster, Saint John, New Brunswick.

Four years later, on September 20, 1905, Estella, age twenty-one, was married to Charles E. Giles, age twenty, by Frank E. Bishop in Lancaster. Estella's two sisters Olive Edna (Williams) Ring and Edith May Williams were the official witnesses to the marriage. Charles E., a "laborer" by trade, was the son of Robert Cameron Giles and Margaret Catherine Kerr. He was born on August 7, 1885 in New River, Charlotte, New Brunswick. There is no record of Estella and Charles E. having any children together.

When the 1911 Census of Canada was taken Estella and Charles E. were recorded as living with his widowed mother in the Parish of Lepreau, Charlotte, New Brunswick. Charles E.'s occupation was listed as "laborer in a saw mill".

The 1921 Census of Canada recorded Estella as once again living with her parents at 39 Havelock Street in Lancaster. Her marital status was listed as "single". It is believed that she and Charles E. divorced as that same year, on July 16, 1921, Charles E. was recorded as crossing the border into the United States and he too listed his marital status as "single". In that "Manifest" Charles E. was described as being 5' 11" tall, weighing 210 pounds, with a medium complexion, dark brown hair and brown eyes.

Sometime around 1930 Charles E. married his second wife Susan Marguerite (Bowlby) Holman. The exact date and place of their marriage has not been found. Susan Marguerite, born in Everett, Middlesex, Massachusetts on August 27, 1893, she was the daughter of John Francis Outhet Bowlby and Eleanor Hawkesworth. Charles E. and Susan Marguerite did not have any children together.

The 1953 and 1965 Urban Preliminary Lists of Electors for the Electoral District of Saint John-Albert recorded Estella as living at 564 Havelock Street in Lancaster.

On July 6, 1968 Charles E. died in Sanford, York, Maine at the age of eighty-two. The cause of his death has not been found. Charles E.'s body was transported back to Massachusetts where he was buried in Lot 98, Grave 4 at the Crocker Park Cemetery in West Barnstable, Barnstable, Massachusetts.

When the 1968 and 1973 Urban Preliminary Lists of Electors for the Electoral District of Saint John-Albert were published, Estella was recorded as still living at 564 Havelock Street in Lancaster. In 1968 she was listed as being a widow.

Estella, at the age of eighty-nine, died on November 27, 1973 "after a period of failing health" at the Saint John General Hospital in Saint John City, Saint John, New Brunswick. At the time of her death she was living at 564 Havelock Street in Lancaster. Her funeral was held at the Castle Funeral Home, 309 Lancaster Avenue, Saint John West, Saint John, New Brunswick at 2:00 on Thursday November 29, 1973. She was buried in the Benjamin Franklin Williams family plot, Avenue 49, Lot 295, in the Old Cedar Hill Cemetery in Saint John West. She has no headstone marking her grave.

SOURCES:

Estella Williams
Birth: (1) Certificate of Registration of Birth, Province of New Brunswick; (2) Index to Late Registration of Births, Microfilm F18772, Provincial Archives of New Brunswick.
Death: (1) Obituary for Estella Williams from the collection of James Harold Williams and Helene Comeau Williams; (2) Listing of Interments prepared by Greenwood Cedar Hill Cemetery Company, Saint John West, Saint John, New Brunswick, November 2012.
Graveyard: Listing of Interments prepared by Greenwood Cedar Hill Cemetery Company, Saint John West, Saint John, New Brunswick, November 2012.

Charles E. Giles
Birth: 1901 Census of Canada, Lepreau, Charlotte, New Brunswick, Page 10.
Marriage: (1) Marriage, Registration Division of Saint John City and County, New Brunswick; (2) Acadia, Canada, Vital and Church Records (Drouin Collection), Saint John, 1891-1907, Schedule B – Marriages, Page 148.
Death: (1) "Maine Death Index, 1960-1996," database, FamilySearch (https://familysearch.org/ark:61903/1.: KCVX-DFP); (2) U.S., Social Security Death Index, 1935-2014 (database on-line), Provo, Utah, USA: Ancestry.com Operations Inc., 2011.
Graveyard: Crocker Park Cemetery Records, West Barnstable, Barnstable, Massachusetts.

Historical Accounts: (1) 1901 Census of Canada, Parish of Lancaster, Saint John, New Brunswick, Page 10; (2) 1901 Census of Canada, Parish of Lepreau, Charlotte, New Brunswick, Page 7; (3) 1911 Census of Canada, Parish of Lepreau, Charlotte, New Brunswick, Page 1; (4) 1921 Census of Canada, Parish of Lancaster, Saint John, New Brunswick, Page 23; (5) U. S. Records of Aliens Pre-Examined in Canada 1917-1954; (6) Canada, Voter Lists, 1953 Urban Preliminary List of Voters, Electoral District of Saint John-Albert, Urban Polling Division No. 179, Parish of Lancaster, Page 2; (7) Canada, Voter Lists, 1965 Urban Preliminary List of Voters, Electoral District of Saint John-Albert, Urban Polling Division No. 194, Parish of Lancaster, Page 2; (8) Canada, Voter Lists, 1968 Urban Preliminary List of Voters, Electoral District of Saint John-Lancaster, Urban Polling Division No. 128, City of Saint John, Page 1; (9) Canada, Voter Lists, 1953 Urban Preliminary List of Voters, Electoral District of Saint John-Lancaster, Urban Polling Division No. 179, City of Saint John, Page 2.

Edith May Williams

(1887 – 1963)

The fifth child of Benjamin Franklin Williams and Jane Brown was Edith May. She was born on May 23, 1887 in Green Head, Saint John, New Brunswick, Canada.

On February 14, 1910, at the age of twenty-two, Edith May was married to Ralph Elmo Coleman, age twenty-eight, in Saint John City, Saint John, New Brunswick by Charles B. Appel. Edith May's sister Olive Edna (Williams) Ring and her husband Frank Ernest Ring served as the official witnesses at the wedding. Ralph Elmo, the son of Emma Coleman and an unknown father, was born on September 17, 1881 in Saint John County, New Brunswick. Emma Coleman's sister, Nancy Jane Coleman, was married to Edith May's uncle, John Nelson Williams.

Edith May and Ralph Elmo had two children during their marriage.

Elsie Gertrude	b. September 1910	d. July 8, 1987
Estella Marion	b. July 26, 1912	d.

In the 1911 Census of Canada Edith May, Ralph Elmo and their first child, Elsie G., were recorded as living at 4 Maberly Street in Lorne Ward, Saint John City, Saint John, New Brunswick. In that census Ralph Elmo's occupation was listed as "station agent".

When the 1921 Census of Canada was taken Edith May, Ralph Elmo and their daughters had moved and were then recorded as living at 5 Metcalf Street in Lorne Ward.

The 1940 Canada Voter List for the Electoral District of Saint John-Albert recorded Edith May, Ralph Elmo (then an "invalid"), their daughter Elsie G. and her husband Harold J. Donkin, and their daughter Estella Marion all living at 5 Metcalf Street in Lorne Ward.

Ralph Elmo died, at the age of sixty-one, at his home on Metcalf Street in Lorne Ward on August 22, 1942. His cause of death was recorded as "vascular renal disease". Ralph Elmo was buried in Lot 300, Avenue 49 at the Old Cedar Hill Cemetery in Saint John West, Saint John, New Brunswick on August 24, 1942.

When the 1945, 1949 and 1957 Voter Lists for the Electoral District of Saint John-Albert were published Edith May was recorded as still living at the family home at 5 Metcalf Street in Lorne Ward.

Edith May outlived her husband by exactly twenty-one years dying at the

Saint John General Hospital in Saint John City on August 22, 1963 at the age of seventy-six. Her cause of death was due to an "acute myocardial infarction". Edith May's funeral was held at 3:00 P.M. on Saturday, August 24, 1963 at Brenan's Funeral Home. She too was buried in lot 300, Avenue 49 at the Old Cedar Hill Cemetery in Saint John West.

Gravestone for Edith May Williams and Ralph Elmo Coleman
(Photograph from the collection of Jeffrey N. Williams and Jacqueline Pon Williams)

SOURCES:

Edith May Williams
Birth: (1) Certificate of Registration of Birth, Province of New Brunswick; (2) Index to Late Registration of Births, Microfilm F18776, Provincial Archives of New Brunswick.
Death: (1) Province of New Brunswick - Registration of Death, Department of Health and Social Services, Saint John City and County Sub-Health District; (2) Listing of Interments prepared by Greenwood Cedar Hill Cemetery Company, Saint John West, Saint John, New Brunswick, September 2016.
Graveyard: (1) Listing of Interments prepared by Greenwood Cedar Hill Cemetery Company, Saint John West, Saint John, New Brunswick, September 2016; (2) Certificate of Registration of Death, County of Saint John, Province of New Brunswick.

Ralph Elmo Coleman
Birth: Province of New Brunswick - Certificate of Registration of Death, Saint John City and County Sub-Health District.
Marriage: (1) Marriage, Registration Division of Saint John City and County, New Brunswick; (2) Acadia, Canada, Vital and Church Records (Drouin Collection), Saint John, Schedule B – Marriages, 1908-1919, Page 35.
Death: (1) Province of New Brunswick - Certificate of Registration of Death, Saint John City and County Sub-Health District; (2) Listing of Interments prepared by Greenwood Cedar Hill Cemetery Company, Saint John West, New Brunswick, September 2016.
Graveyard: (1) Listing of Interments prepared by Greenwood Cedar Hill Cemetery Company, Saint John West, Saint John, New Brunswick, September 2016; (2) Province of New Brunswick - Certificate of Registration of Death, Saint John City and County Sub-Health District.

Historical Accounts: (1) 1901 Census of Canada, Parish of Lancaster, Saint John, New Brunswick, Page 10; (2) 1911 Census of Canada, Lorne Ward, Saint John City, Saint John, New Brunswick, Page 7; (3) 1921 Census of Canada, Lorne Ward, Saint John City, Saint John, New Brunswick, Page 16; (4) 1940 - Canada, Voters List for the Electoral District of Saint John-Albert, Urban Polling Division 10, Page 1; (5) 1945 - Canada, Voter Lists for the Electoral District of Saint John-Albert, Urban Polling Division 10, Page 1; (6) 1949 - Canada, Voter Lists for the Electoral District of Saint John-Albert, Urban Polling Division 10, Page 1; (7) 1957 - Canada, Voter Lists for the Electoral District of Saint John-Albert, Urban Polling Division 12, Page 1.

Charles Seeley Williams

(1890 – 1960)

Charles Seeley, the sixth child of Benjamin Franklin Williams and Jane Brown was born in Randolph, Saint John, New Brunswick, Canada on January 24, 1890.

When the 1911 Census of Canada was taken Charles Seeley, age twenty, was recorded as living with his parents on George Street in Fairville, Saint John, New Brunswick and working as a "railroad laborer".

At the age of twenty-eight Charles Seeley was married to the widow Ethel May (Logan) Moyer, age twenty-five, on January 20, 1919 at Saint Stephens, Charlotte, New Brunswick by Henry Strathard, a clergyman. Ethel May, the daughter of Charles T. Logan and Mary Agnes O'Brien, was born on February 8, 1893 in Boston, Suffolk, Massachusetts. At the time of their marriage Charles Seeley became the stepfather to two boys, Homer and James Moyer, from Ethel May's first marriage.

During their marriage Charles Seeley and Ethel May had six additional children together.

Shirley Irene	b. November 23, 1919	d. October 7, 2012
Olive Mae	b. March 11, 1921	d. September 20, 1977
Dorothy Silverdore	b. April 3, 1923	d. March 18, 2008
Charles Allingham	b. 1926	d.
Garnet Donald	b. 1930	d. July 10, 1992
Infant Boy	*b.*	*d.*

The gravestone for Charles Seeley and Ethel May indicates that they are buried with an "infant son". No record has been found regarding the birth and death of that child.

In the 1921 Census of Canada Charles Seeley, Ethel May and their children were recorded as living at 39 Havelock Street in Lancaster, Saint John, New Brunswick. In that census Charles Seeley was working as an "engineer".

The 1949 Canada Voter List for the Electoral District of Saint John-Albert published on June 13th of that year recorded Charles Seeley, Ethel May, their son Charles Allingham and his wife, and their daughter Shirley Irene as living at 149 Winslow Street, Saint John West, Saint John, New Brunswick.

Ethel May died on August 4, 1949 at the age of fifty-six at St. Joseph's Hospital in Saint John City, Saint John, New Brunswick of an "intestinal obstruction". On August 6, 1949 Ethel May was buried in Section C, Lot 42 E1/2, Grave 2 at the Cedar Hill Extension Cemetery in Saint John West.

On December 13, 1952, a little more than three years after his first wife's death, Charles Seeley, then age sixty-two, was married to his second wife Edith Barbara Galbraith, age forty-nine, by Reverend John Humphreys at the Y.W.C.A. in Saint John City. Edith Barbara's brother Allison Herbert Galbraith and his wife Olive Daisy Clancy Galbraith served as the official witnesses to her marriage. The daughter of Herbert John and Laura Jane Galbraith, Edith Barbara was born on August 21, 1903 in Lorneville, Saint John, New Brunswick. At the time of their wedding Charles Seeley was working as an "engineer" for the Canadian Pacific Railroad and Edith Barbara was a "cook" at the Provincial Hospital in Saint John West. There is no record of Charles Seeley and Edith Barbara as ever having had any children together.

When the 1957 Voter List for the Electoral District of Saint John-Albert was published Charles Seeley, then "retired", and Edith Barbara were listed as living at 19 Prince William Street in Lancaster.

At the age of seventy Charles Seeley died of "thyroid cancer" on November 18, 1960 at the Saint John General Hospital in Saint John City. At the time of his death he was still living at 19 Prince William Street in Lancaster. Charles Seeley was buried with his first wife Ethel May in Section C, Lot 42 E1/2, Grave 1 at the Cedar Hill Extension Cemetery in Saint John West.

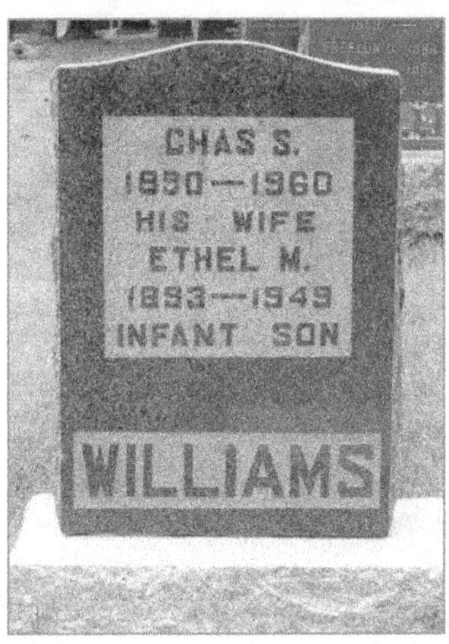

Gravestone for Charles Seeley Williams and Ethel May Logan
(Photograph from the collection of Jeffrey N. Williams and Jacqueline Pon Williams)

Outliving her husband by almost eleven years, Edith Barbara died "after a short illness" at St. Joseph's Hospital in Saint John City on October 27, 1971 at the age of sixty-eight. Her funeral was held at 2:00 P.M. on Friday, October 29,

1971 at the Calvin Funeral Home in Saint John West. At the time of her death Edith Barbara was living at 556 Tilton Avenue, Saint John West. She was buried in her parents' plot in Row 2, Lot 70, Grave 2 off of the Derryogue Road access lane at the Lorneville Cemetery in Lorneville.

Gravestone for Edith Barbara Galbraith
(Photograph from the collection of Jeffrey N. Williams and Jacqueline Pon Williams)

SOURCES:

Charles Seeley Williams
Birth: : (1) Province of New Brunswick, Department of Health, Certificate of Registration of Birth, Saint John City and County Sub-Health District; (2) Index to Late Registration of Births, Microfilm F18780, Provincial Archives of New Brunswick; (3) Acadia, Canada, Vital and Church Records (Drouin Collection), Saint John, 1888-1895, Page 203.
Death: Province of New Brunswick - Registration of Death, Department of Health and Social Services, Saint John City and County Sub-Health District.
Graveyard: (1) Listing of Interments prepared by Greenwood Cedar Hill Cemetery Company, Saint John West, Saint John, New Brunswick, November 2012; (2) Province of New Brunswick - Registration of Death, Department of Health and Social Services, Saint John City and County Sub-Health District.

Ethel May Logan
Birth: Certificate of Registration of Death, Saint John City and County, Province of New Brunswick.
Marriage: Marriage Return, Registration Division of Charlotte County, New Brunswick.
Death: Certificate of Registration of Death, Saint John City and County, Province of New Brunswick.
Graveyard: (1) Listing of Interments prepared by Greenwood Cedar Hill Cemetery Company, Saint John West, Saint John, New Brunswick, November 2012; (2) Certificate of Registration of Death, Saint John City and County, Province of New Brunswick.

Infant Boy Williams
Birth:
Death:
Graveyard: Gravestone.

Edith Barbara Galbraith
Birth: (1) Births, Registration Division of Saint John City and County, New Brunswick; (2) Acadia, Canada, Vital and Church Records (Drouin Collection), Saint John, 1899-1905, Schedule A – Births, Page 140.
Marriage: Province of New Brunswick, Department of Health, Official Notice of Marriage, Saint John City and County Sub-Health District.
Death: Obituary, Evening Times Globe, Thursday, October 28, 1971, Page 38.
Graveyard: (1) Lorneville Cemetery Records, Lorneville, Saint John, New Brunswick; (2) "Listing of Interments for the Lorneville Cemetery, Lorneville, Saint John, New Brunswick", transcribed by Suzanne Lisson, May 6, 1996; (3) Obituary, Evening Times Globe, Thursday, October 28, 1971, Page 38.

Historical Accounts: (1) 1911 Census of Canada, Parish of Lancaster, Saint John, New Brunswick, Page 23; (2) 1921 Census of Canada, Parish of Lancaster, Saint John, New Brunswick, Page 23; (3) 1949 Canada Voter List for the Electoral District of Saint John-Albert, Urban Polling Division 128, Page 1; (4) 1957 Canada Voter List for the Electoral District of Saint John-Albert, City of Lancaster, Urban Polling Division 194, Page 2

Frederick John Williams

(1894 – 1955)

The seventh child, Frederick John, of Benjamin Franklin Williams and Jane Brown was born in South Bay, Saint John, New Brunswick, Canada on September 18, 1894.

In the 1911and 1921 Census' of Canada Frederick John was recorded as living with his parents at 39 Havelock Street in Lancaster, Saint John, New Brunswick. In the 1911 census his occupation was listed as a "railroad laborer" and in the 1921 census as a "railroad fireman".

On December 11, 1926, at the age of thirty-two, Frederick John was married to Elizabeth Jean Fraser age thirty-five at 35 Havelock Street in Lancaster. Official witnesses for the ceremony were Frederick John's brother and sister, John Garnett Williams and Estella (Williams) Giles. Born in Newton Stewart, Dumfries and Galloway, Scotland on October 26, 1889, Elizabeth Jean was the daughter of William Fraser and Mary Jane Kean. There is no record of Frederick John and Elizabeth Jean ever having any children during their marriage.

In the 1940 Rural Preliminary List of Electors for the Electoral District of Saint John-Albert, Frederick John and Elizabeth Jean were listed as living at 37 Champlain Street in Lancaster.

Elizabeth Jane died on January 10, 1955 at the Saint John General Hospital in Saint John City, Saint John, New Brunswick at age sixty-five. Her cause of death was listed as "myocarditis".

That same day, January 10, 1955, also at the Saint John General Hospital, Frederick John, age sixty, died of a "self-inflicted gunshot to the head". From the records available it appears that Frederick John shot himself after his wife had died.

At the time of their deaths Elizabeth Jane and Frederick John were living at 302 King Street in Saint John West, Saint John, New Brunswick and Frederick John was working as a "locomotive engineer" for the Canadian Pacific Railway, as he had for thirty-seven years.

Funerals for Frederick John and Elizabeth Jane were held at the Ross Funeral Home in Saint John West on Thursday, January 13, 1955. They were both buried at the Cedar Hill Extension Cemetery in Saint John West in Section G, Lot 54 E1/2 in Graves 7 & 8.

SOURCES:

Frederick John Williams
Birth: (1) Certificate of Registration of Birth, Province of New Brunswick; (2) Index to Late Registration of Births, Microfilm F18785, Provincial Archives of New Brunswick.
Death: (1) Province of New Brunswick - Registration of Death, Saint John City and County Sub-Health District; (2) Listing of Interments prepared by Greenwood Cedar Hill Cemetery Company, Saint John West, Saint John, New Brunswick, November 2012; (3) Death Notice, Saint John Telegraph-Journal.
Graveyard: (1) Listing of Interments prepared by Greenwood Cedar Hill Cemetery Company, Saint John West, Saint John, New Brunswick, November 2012; (2) Province of New Brunswick - Registration of Death, Saint John City and County Sub-Health District.

Elizabeth Jane Fraser
Birth: Province of New Brunswick - Registration of Death, Saint John City and County Sub-Health District.
Marriage: Province of New Brunswick, Department of Health, Official Notice of Marriage, Saint John City and County Sub-Health District.
Death: (1) Province of New Brunswick - Registration of Death, Saint John City and County Sub-Health District; (2) Listing of Interments prepared by Greenwood Cedar Hill Cemetery Company, Saint John West, Saint John, New Brunswick, November 2012; (3) Death Notice, Saint John Telegraph-Journal.
Graveyard: (1) Listing of Interments prepared by Greenwood Cedar Hill Cemetery Company, Saint John West, Saint John, New Brunswick, November 2012; (2) Province of New Brunswick - Registration of Death, Saint John City and County Sub-Health District.

Historical Accounts: (1) 1911 Census of Canada, Lancaster, Saint John, New Brunswick, Page 23; (2) 1921 Census of Canada, Lancaster, Saint John, New Brunswick, Page 2; (3) 1940 Rural Preliminary List of Electors for the Electoral District of Saint John-Albert, Rural Polling Division 144B, Page 2.

Person Index

Person Index

www.ingramcontent.com/pod-product-compliance
Lightning Source LLC
Chambersburg PA
CBHW070252290326
41930CB00041B/2467
9780578194790